BUILDING BLOCKS OF ENGLISH

ADJECTIVES, ADVERBS, AND OTHER PARTS OF SPEECH

Written by Fred Maxon

Illustrated by Ruth Bennett

a Scott Fetzer company
Chicago

This edition is co-published by agreement between World Book, Inc. and Cherry Lake Publishing Group

World Book, Inc.
180 North LaSalle Street
Suite 900
Chicago, Illinois 60601
USA

Cherry Lake Publishing Group
2395 South Huron Parkway
Suite 200
Ann Arbor, MI 48104
USA

© 2024. All rights reserved. This volume may not be reproduced in whole or in part in any form without prior written permission from the publisher.

WORLD BOOK and the GLOBE DEVICE are registered trademarks or trademarks of World Book, Inc.

WORLD BOOK STAFF

Editorial

Vice President
Tom Evans

Senior Manager, New Content
Jeff De La Rosa

Curriculum Designer
Caroline Davidson

Proofreader
Nathalie Strassheim

Graphics and Design

Senior Visual Communications Designer
Melanie Bender

Library of Congress Control Number: 2024936277

Building Blocks of English
ISBN: 978-0-7166-5517-6 (set, hardcover)

Adjectives, Adverbs, and Other Parts of Speech
ISBN: 978-0-7166-5525-1 (hardcover)

Also available as:
ISBN: 978-0-7166-5535-0 (e-book)

Cherry Lake ISBNs

Building Blocks of English
ISBN: 978-0-7166-8821-1 (set, softcover)

Adjectives, Adverbs, and Other Parts of Speech
ISBN: 978-0-7166-8797-9 (softcover)

Printed in the United States of America

Acknowledgments:
Writer: Fred Maxon
Illustrator: Ruth Bennett/The Bright Agency
Series Advisor: Marjorie Frank

TABLE OF CONTENTS

The Story So Far...	4
Adjectives	6
Comparing With Adjectives	12
Articles	18
Adverbs	26
Prepositions	30
Interjections	36
Show What You Know	38
Answers and Words to Know	40

There is a glossary on page 40. Terms defined in the glossary are in type **that looks like this** on their first appearance.

THE STORY SO FAR...

Once upon a time, there was a poor boy. His name was Tommy Pail. Tommy lived in a faraway place called Booktown.

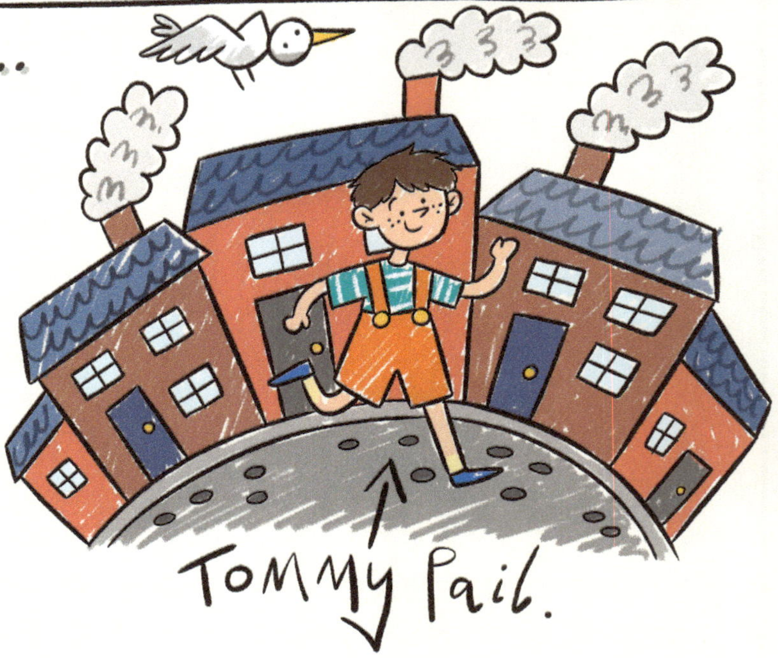
Tommy Pail.

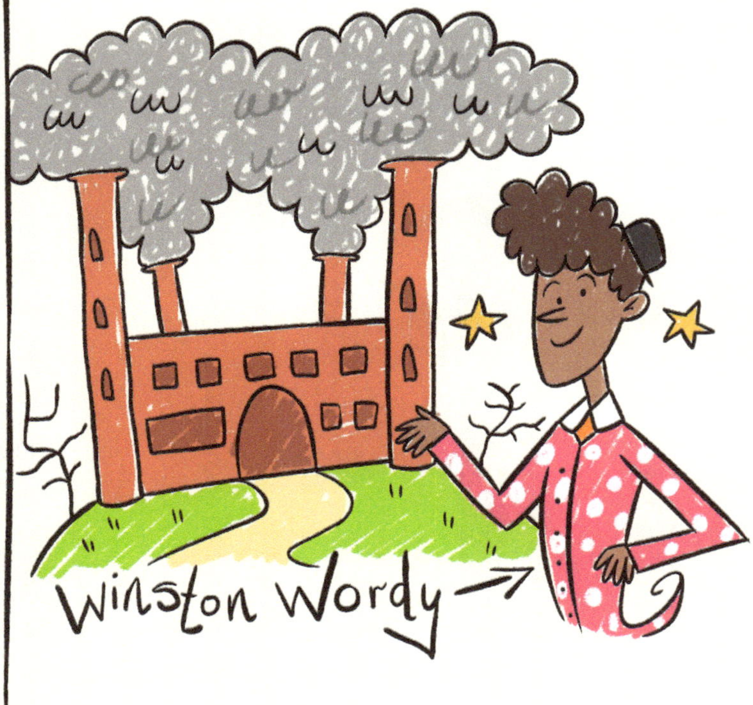
Winston Wordy

But Tommy's luck was about to change. He won a tour of the nearby sentence factory. It was owned by the famous writer Winston Wordy.

The other children on the tour did not pay attention to Winston Wordy. They misbehaved and got into all sorts of trouble.

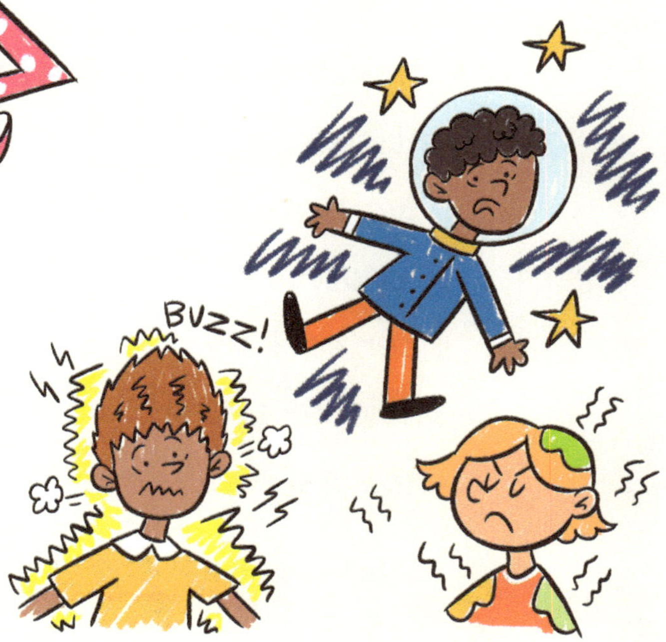
BUZZ!

Person

Place

Thing

Tommy, however, listened carefully to every word. He wanted to become a great writer, too. Tommy learned that a **noun** is a person, place, or thing.

He learned that a **verb** is a word that describes an action or a state of being. By the end of the tour, Tommy was the only child who had not fallen to mischief.

Winston Wordy rewarded Tommy for his good behavior. He named Tommy heir to the sentence factory. One day, this would all belong to him.

ADJECTIVES

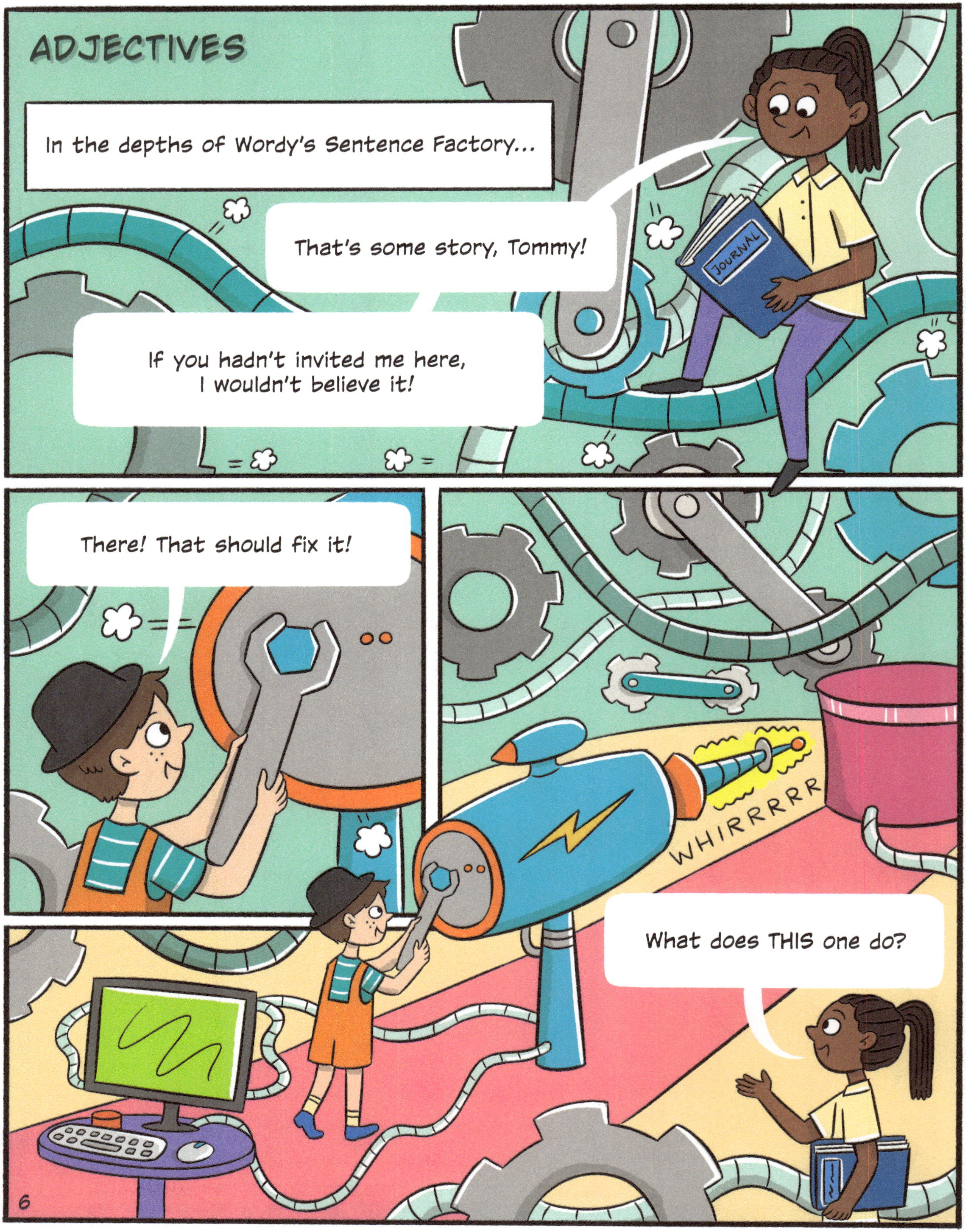
In the depths of Wordy's Sentence Factory...
That's some story, Tommy!
If you hadn't invited me here, I wouldn't believe it!
There! That should fix it!
WHIRRRRR
What does THIS one do?
JOURNAL

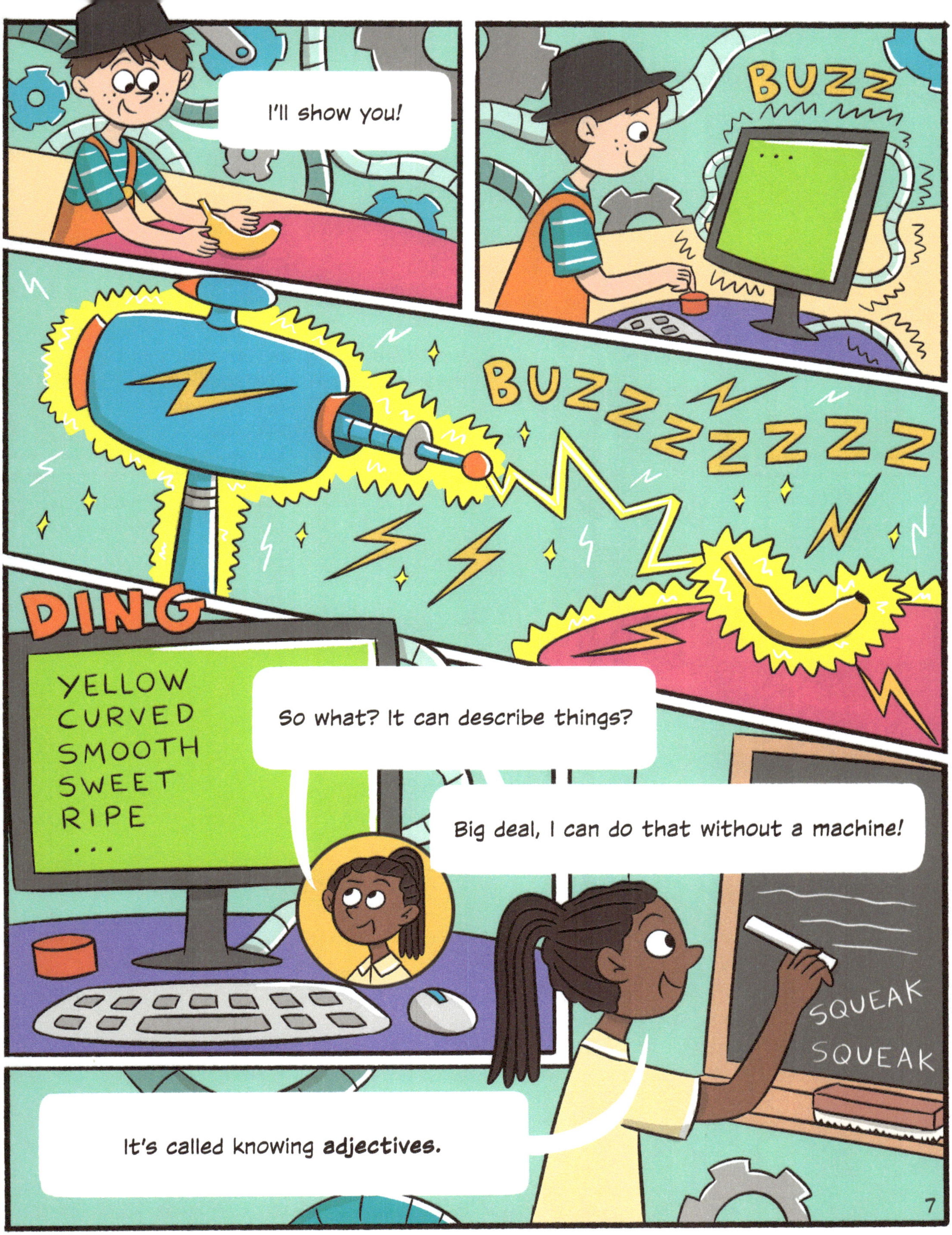
I'll show you!
BUZZ
...
BUZZZZZZZZ
DING
YELLOW
CURVED
SMOOTH
SWEET
RIPE
...
So what? It can describe things?
Big deal, I can do that without a machine!
SQUEAK
SQUEAK
It's called knowing **adjectives**.

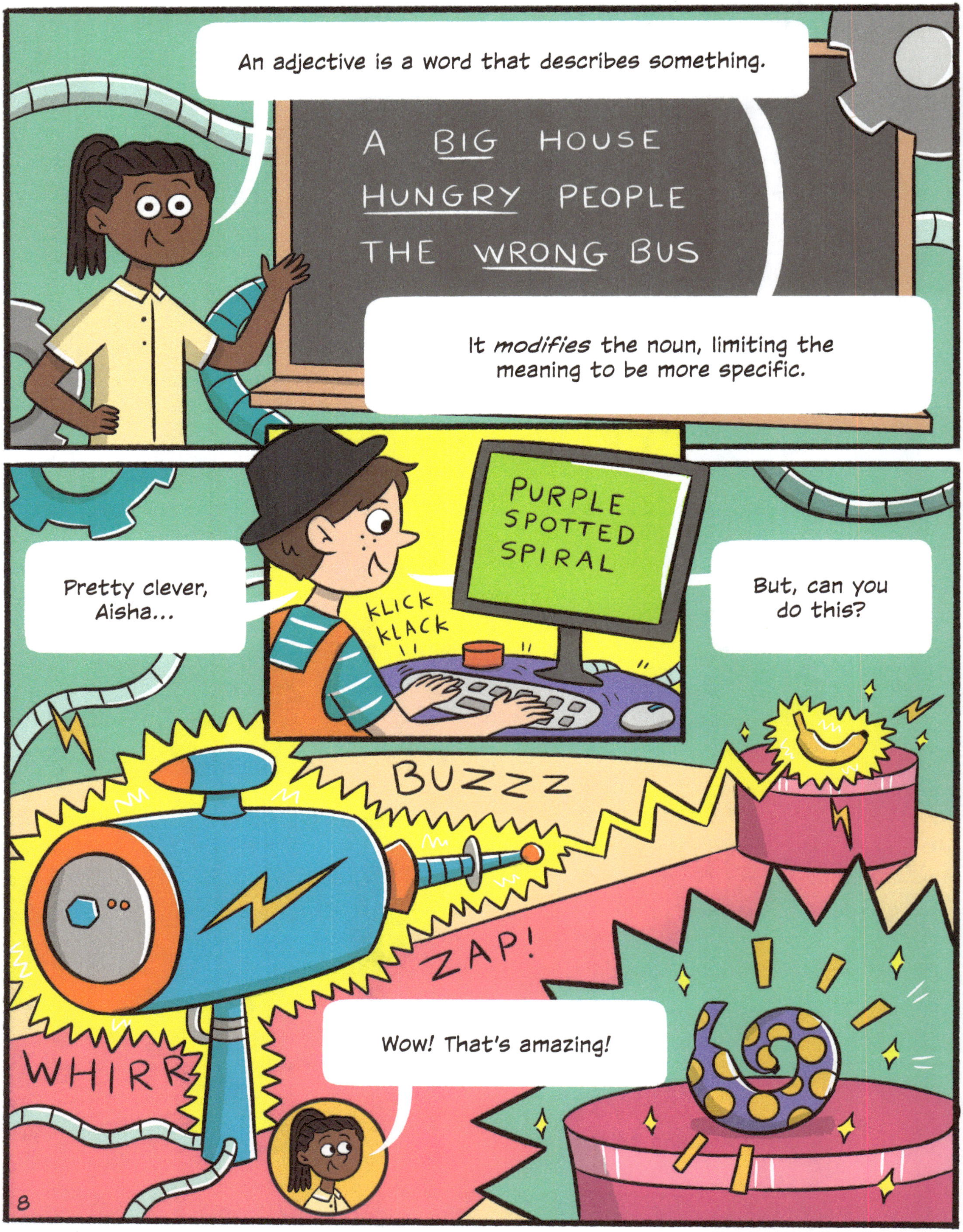
An adjective is a word that describes something.
A BIG HOUSE
HUNGRY PEOPLE
THE WRONG BUS
It *modifies* the noun, limiting the meaning to be more specific.
Pretty clever, Aisha...
PURPLE SPOTTED SPIRAL
KLICK KLACK
But, can you do this?
BUZZZ
ZAP!
WHIRR
Wow! That's amazing!

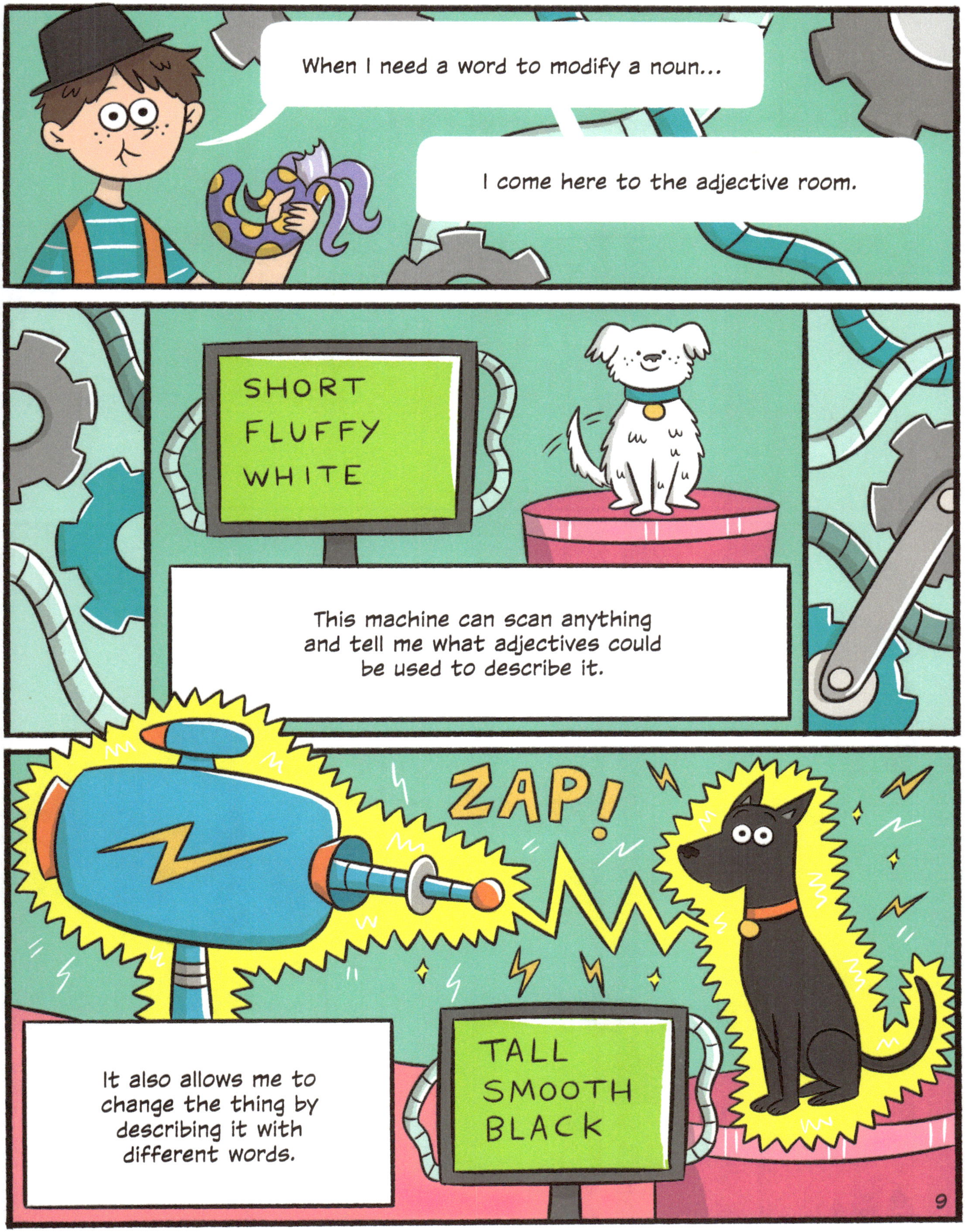
When I need a word to modify a noun...
I come here to the adjective room.
SHORT
FLUFFY
WHITE
This machine can scan anything and tell me what adjectives could be used to describe it.
ZAP!
It also allows me to change the thing by describing it with different words.
TALL
SMOOTH
BLACK

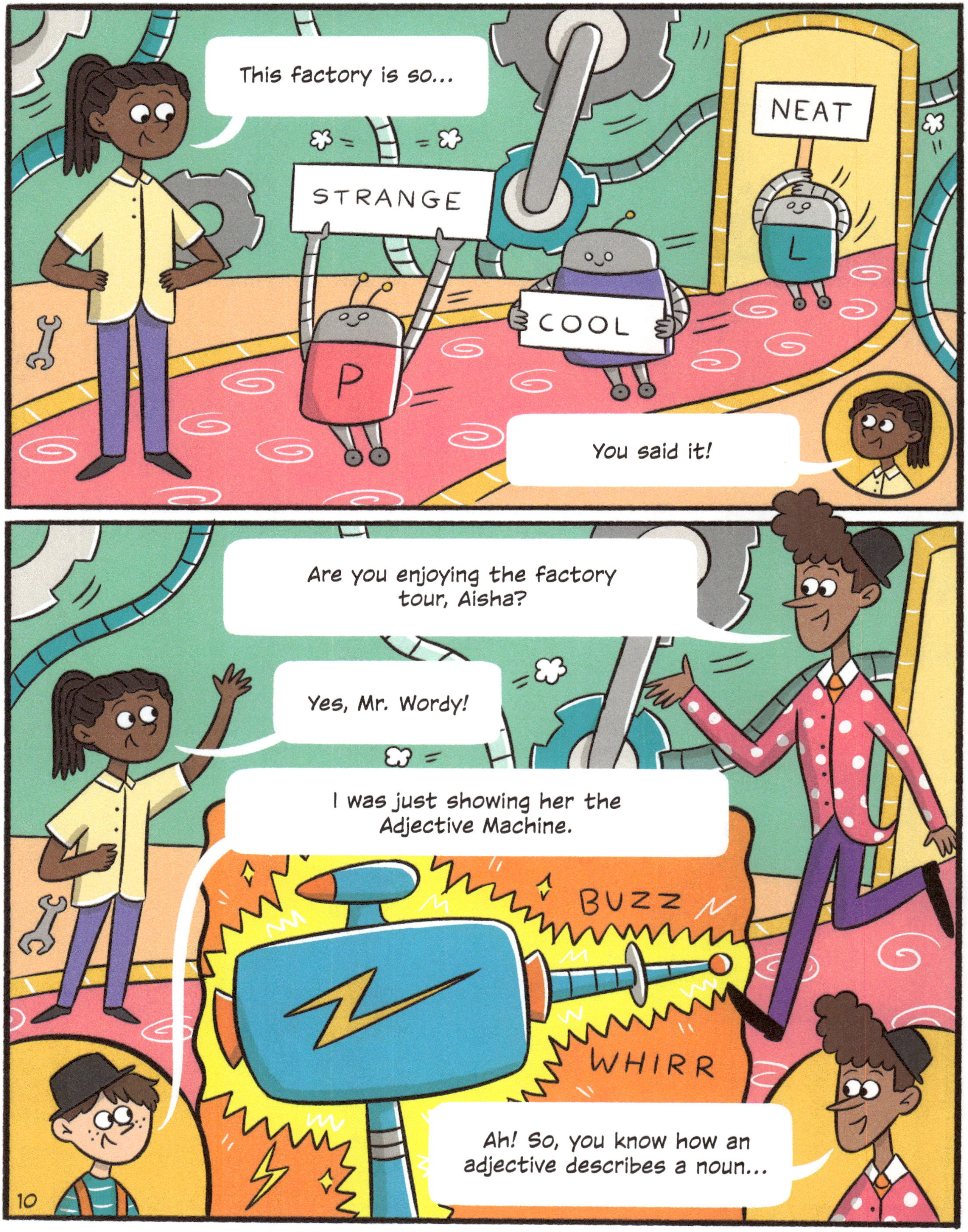
This factory is so...
STRANGE
P
COOL
NEAT
L
You said it!
Are you enjoying the factory tour, Aisha?
Yes, Mr. Wordy!
I was just showing her the Adjective Machine.
BUZZ
WHIRR
Ah! So, you know how an adjective describes a noun...

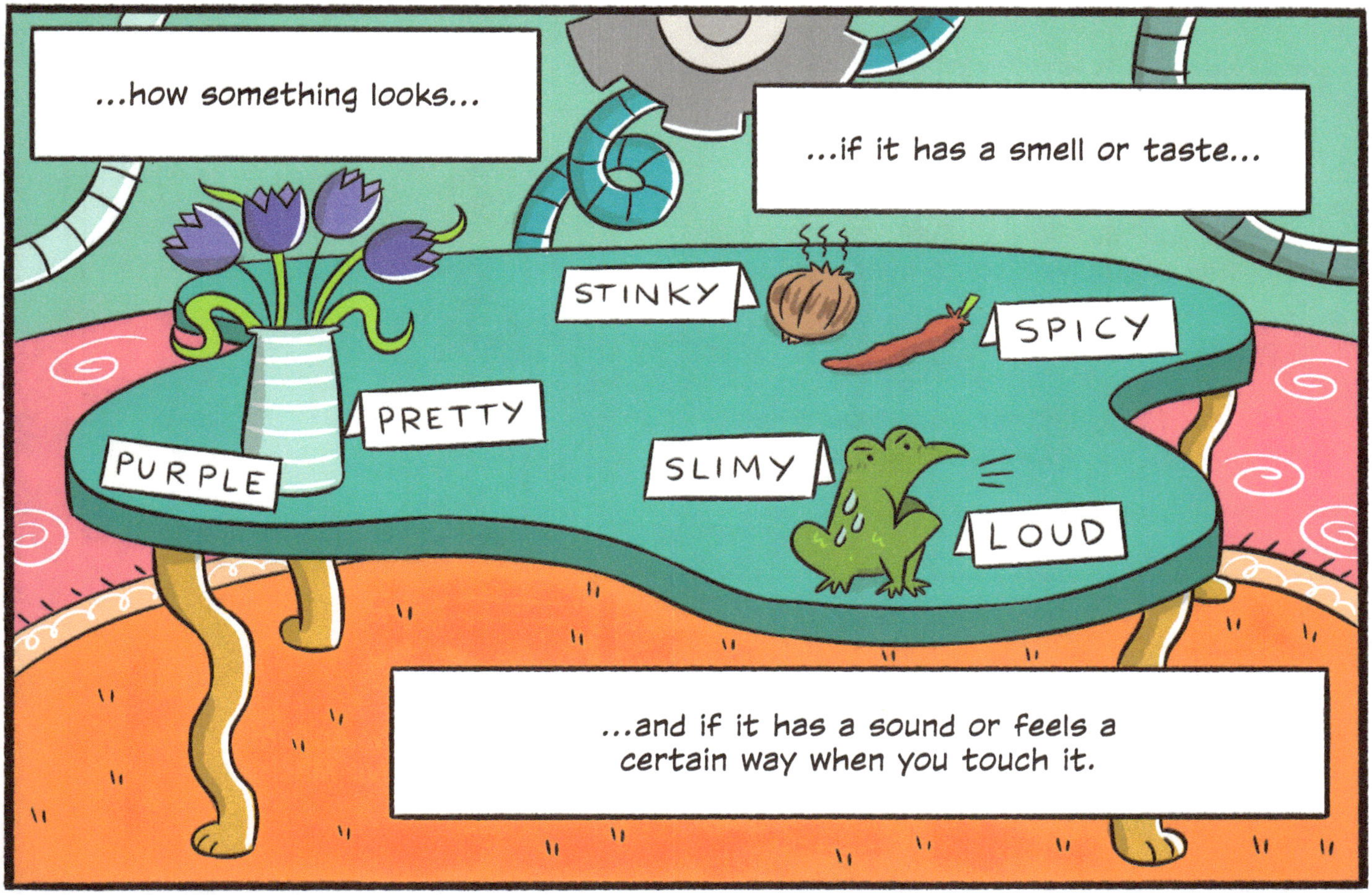
...how something looks...
...if it has a smell or taste...
STINKY
SPICY
PRETTY
PURPLE
SLIMY
LOUD
...and if it has a sound or feels a certain way when you touch it.

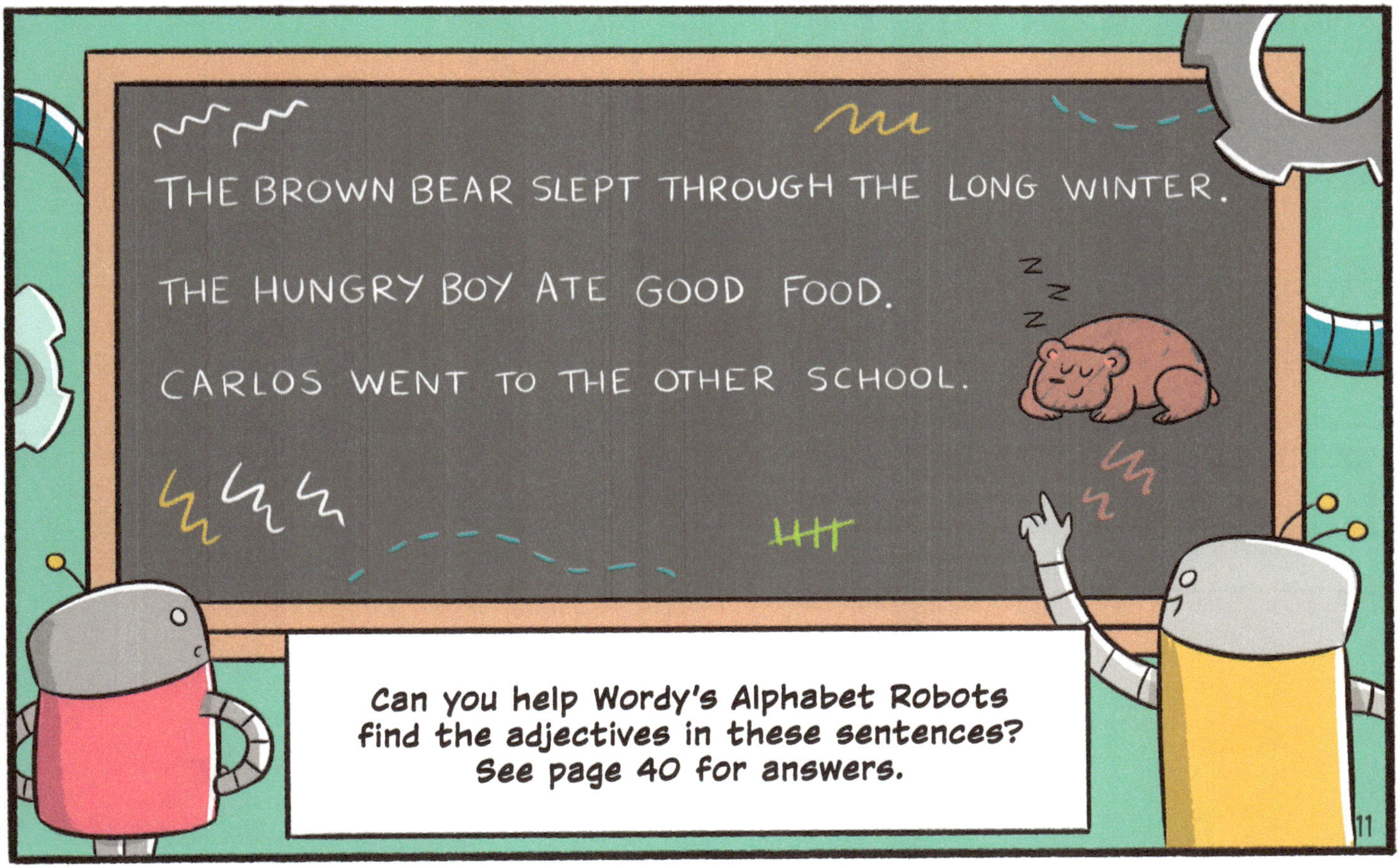
THE BROWN BEAR SLEPT THROUGH THE LONG WINTER.
THE HUNGRY BOY ATE GOOD FOOD.
CARLOS WENT TO THE OTHER SCHOOL.
Can you help Wordy's Alphabet Robots find the adjectives in these sentences? See page 40 for answers.

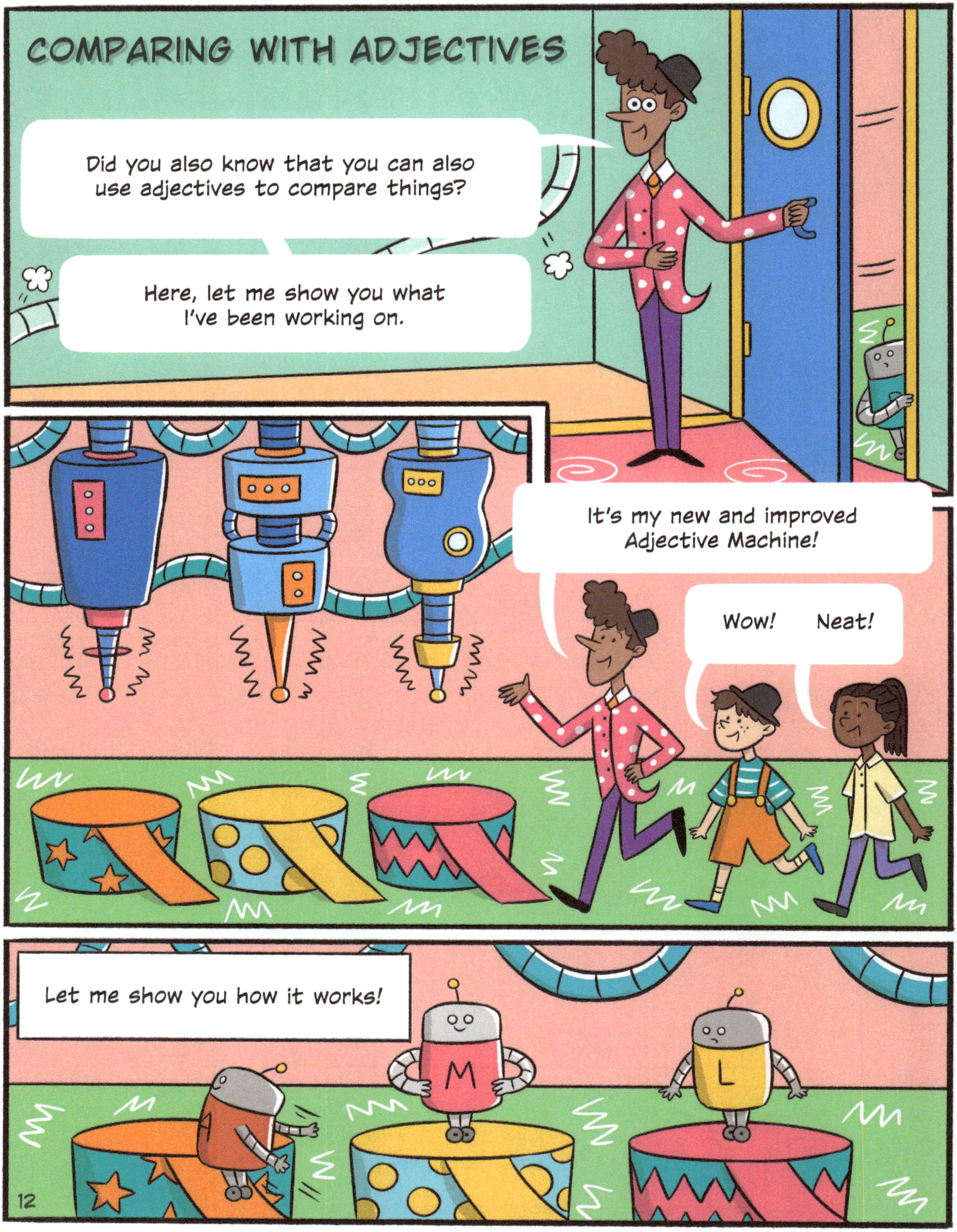
COMPARING WITH ADJECTIVES
Did you also know that you can also use adjectives to compare things?
Here, let me show you what I've been working on.
It's my new and improved Adjective Machine!
Wow!
Neat!
Let me show you how it works!
M
L

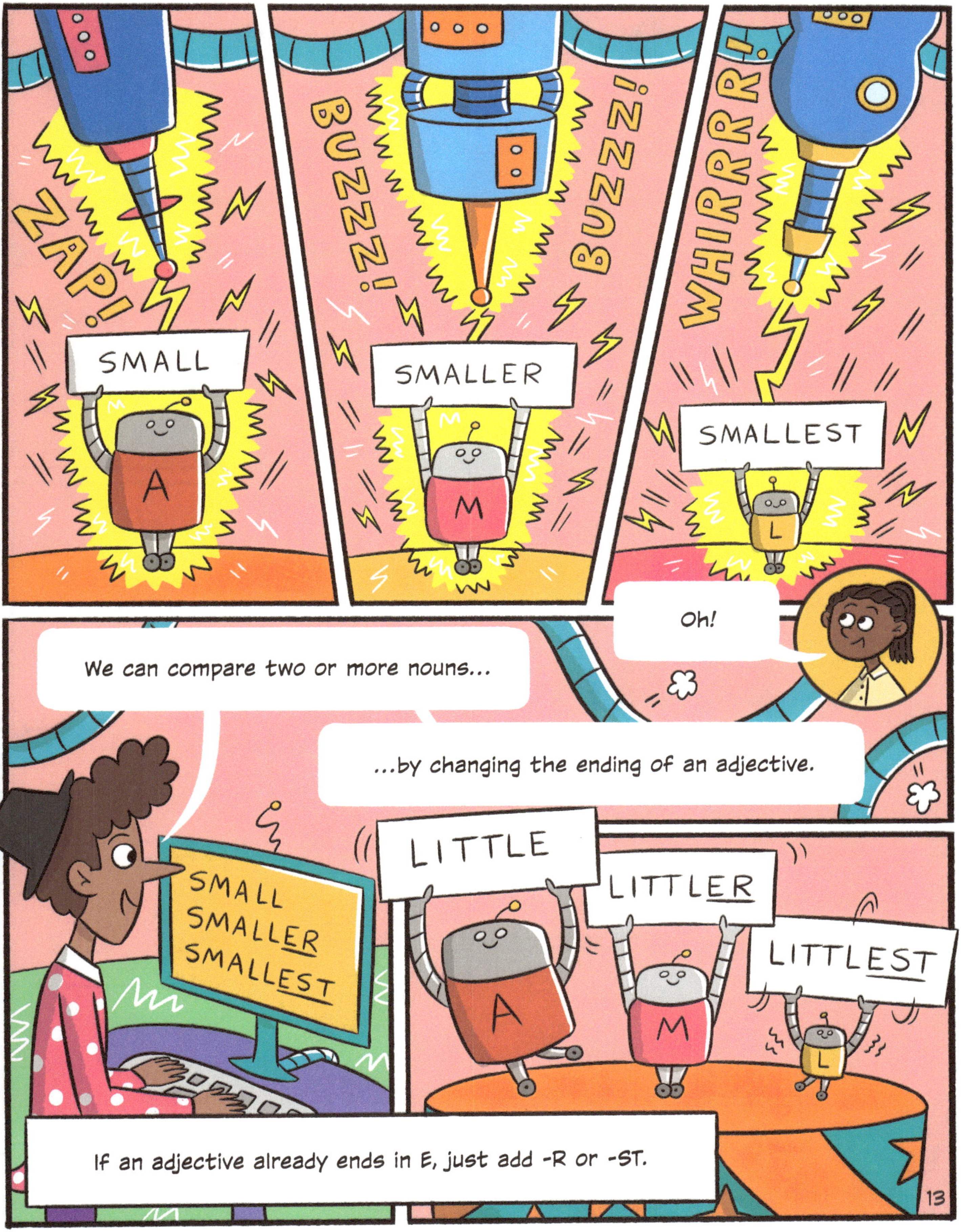
ZAP!
SMALL
A
BUZZZ! BUZZZ!
SMALLER
M
WHIRRRR!
SMALLEST
L
Oh!
We can compare two or more nouns...
...by changing the ending of an adjective.
SMALL
SMALLER
SMALLEST
LITTLE
LITTLER
LITTLEST
A
M
L
If an adjective already ends in E, just add -R or -ST.

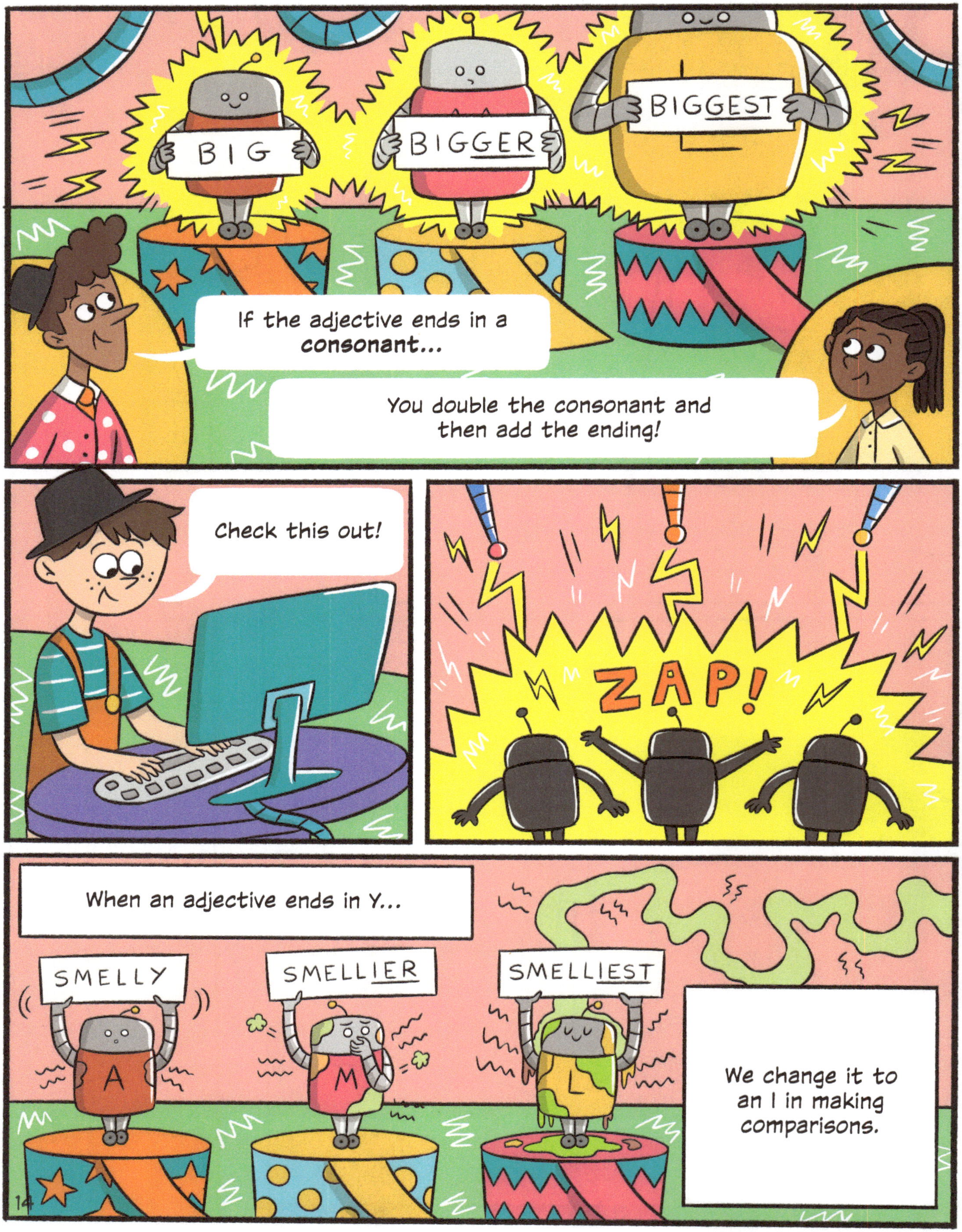
BIG
BIGGER
BIGGEST
If the adjective ends in a **consonant**...
You double the consonant and then add the ending!
Check this out!
ZAP!
When an adjective ends in Y...
SMELLY
SMELLIER
SMELLIEST
We change it to an I in making comparisons.

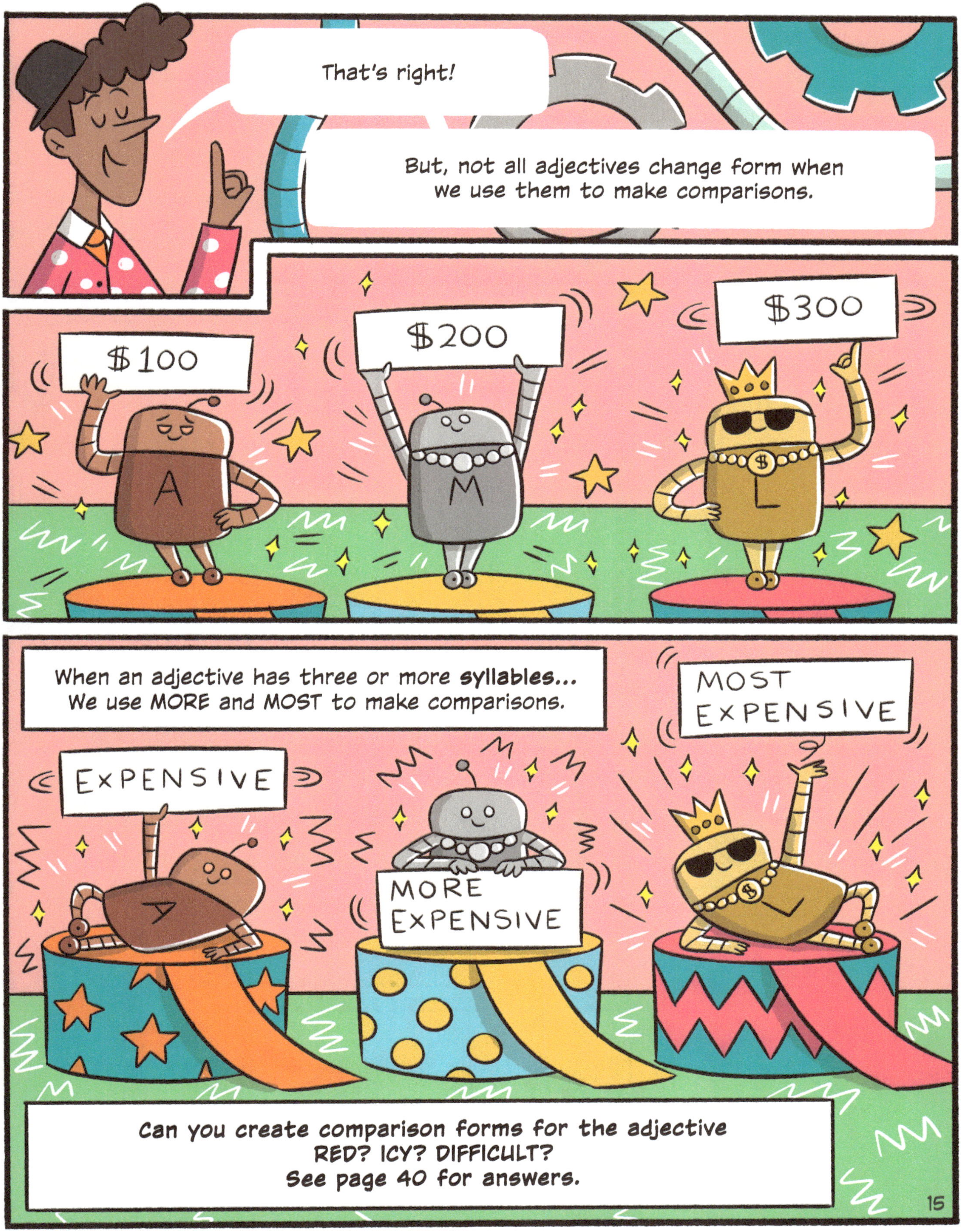

That's right!
But, not all adjectives change form when we use them to make comparisons.
$100
$200
$300
A
M
L
When an adjective has three or more **syllables...** We use MORE and MOST to make comparisons.
MOST EXPENSIVE
EXPENSIVE
MORE EXPENSIVE
Can you create comparison forms for the adjective RED? ICY? DIFFICULT?
See page 40 for answers.

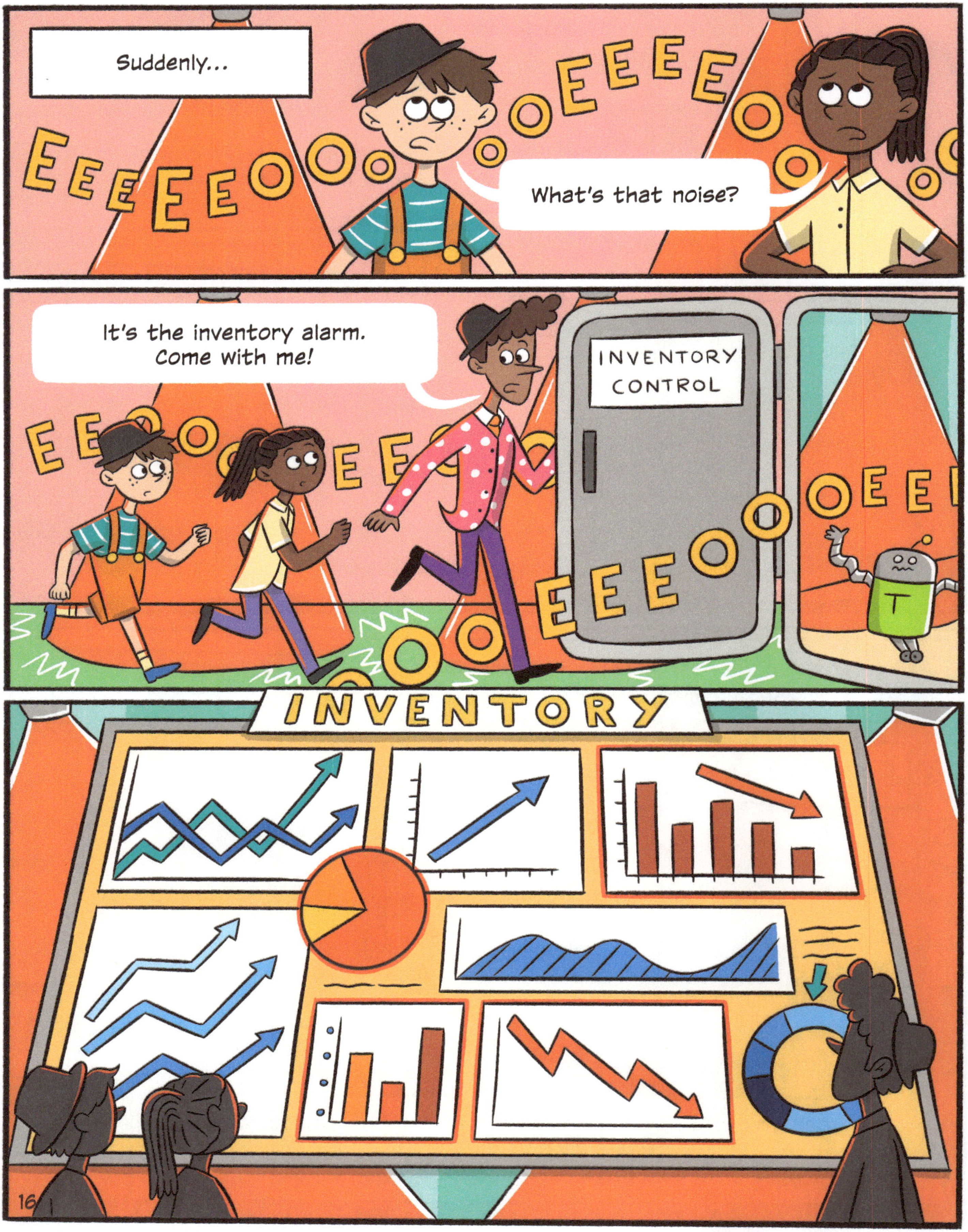
Suddenly...
What's that noise?
It's the inventory alarm. Come with me!
INVENTORY CONTROL
INVENTORY

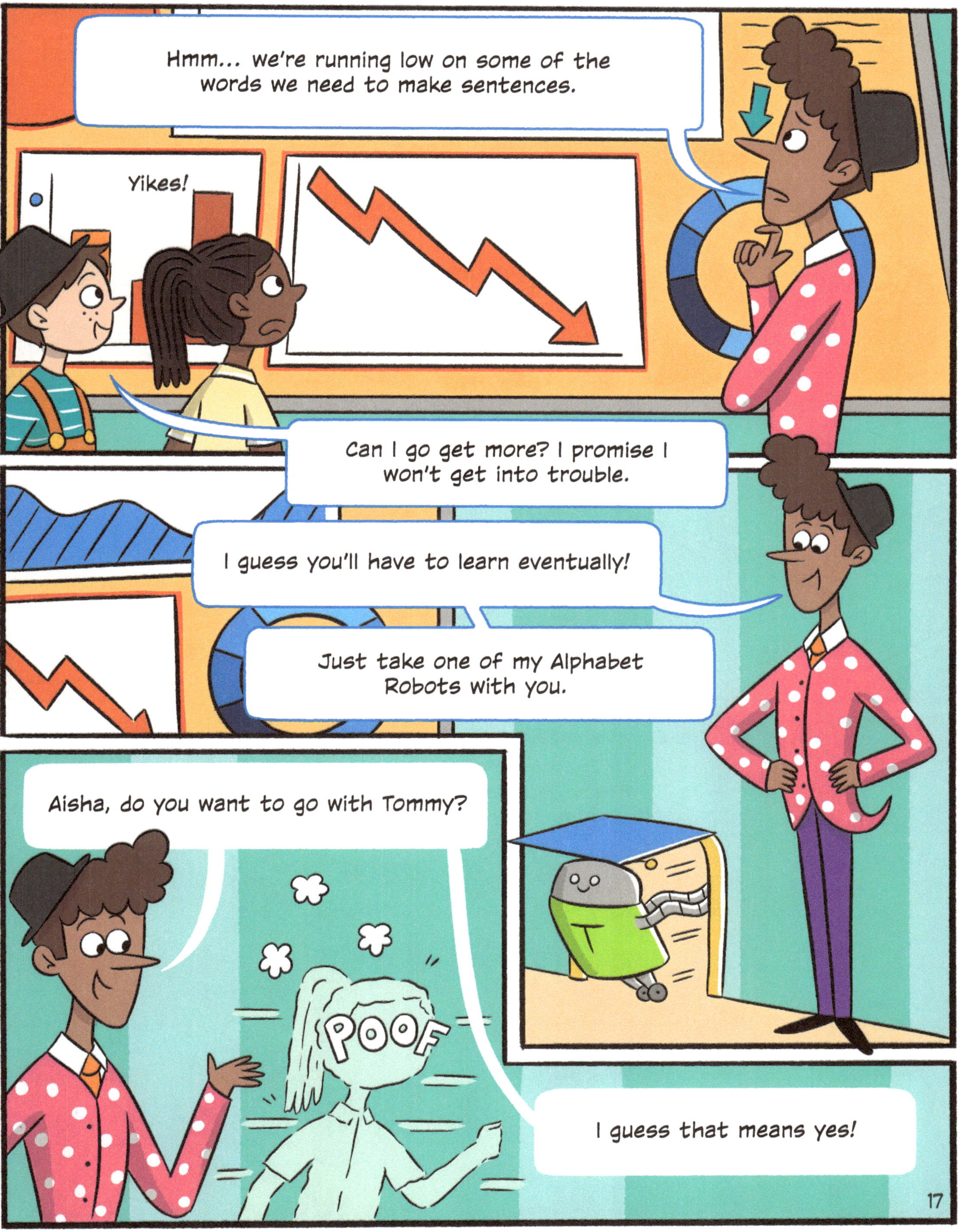
Hmm... we're running low on some of the words we need to make sentences.
Yikes!
Can I go get more? I promise I won't get into trouble.
I guess you'll have to learn eventually!
Just take one of my Alphabet Robots with you.
Aisha, do you want to go with Tommy?
POOF
I guess that means yes!

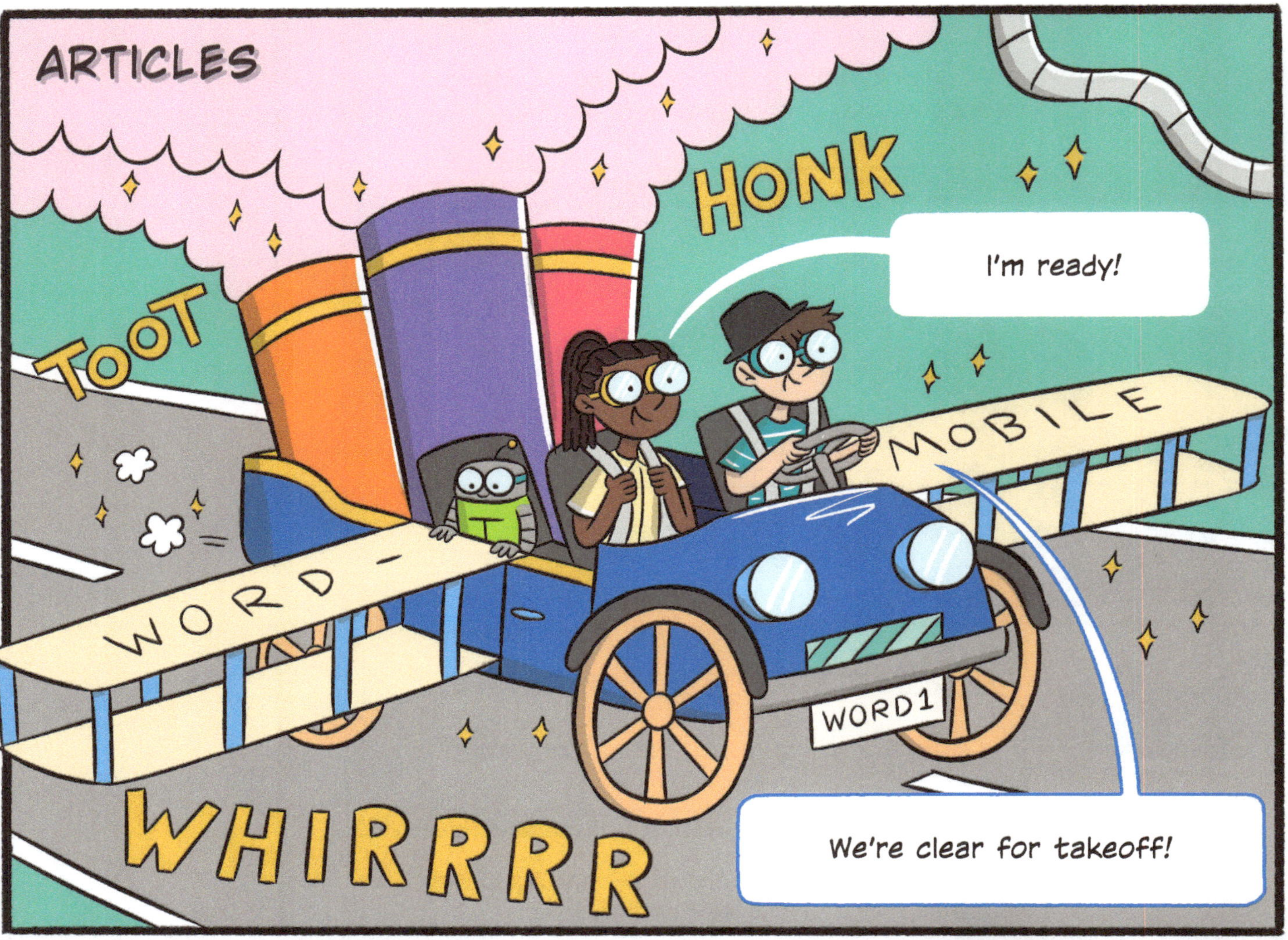
ARTICLES
TOOT
HONK
I'm ready!
WORD-MOBILE
WORD1
WHIRRRR
We're clear for takeoff!

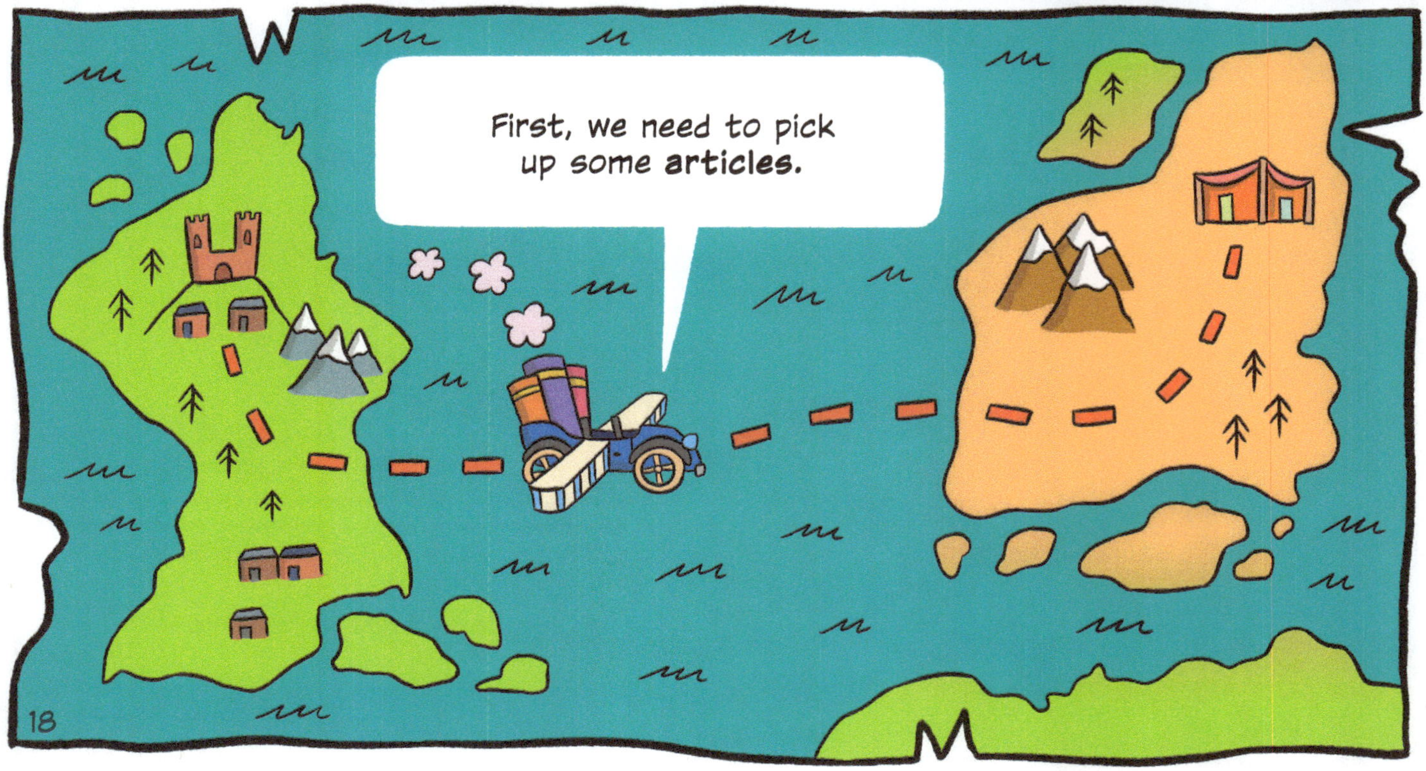
First, we need to pick up some **articles.**

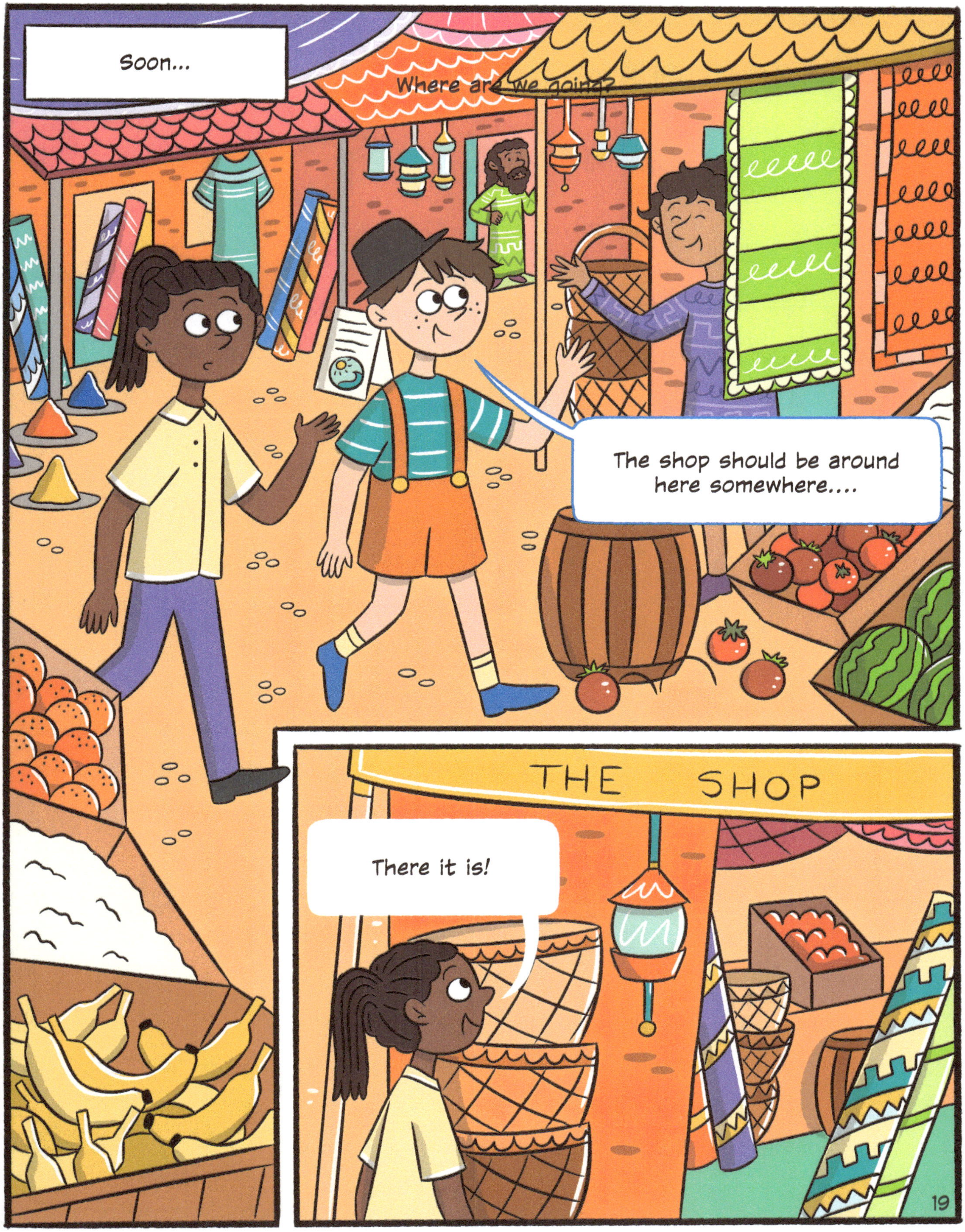
Soon...
Where are we going?
The shop should be around here somewhere....
THE SHOP
There it is!

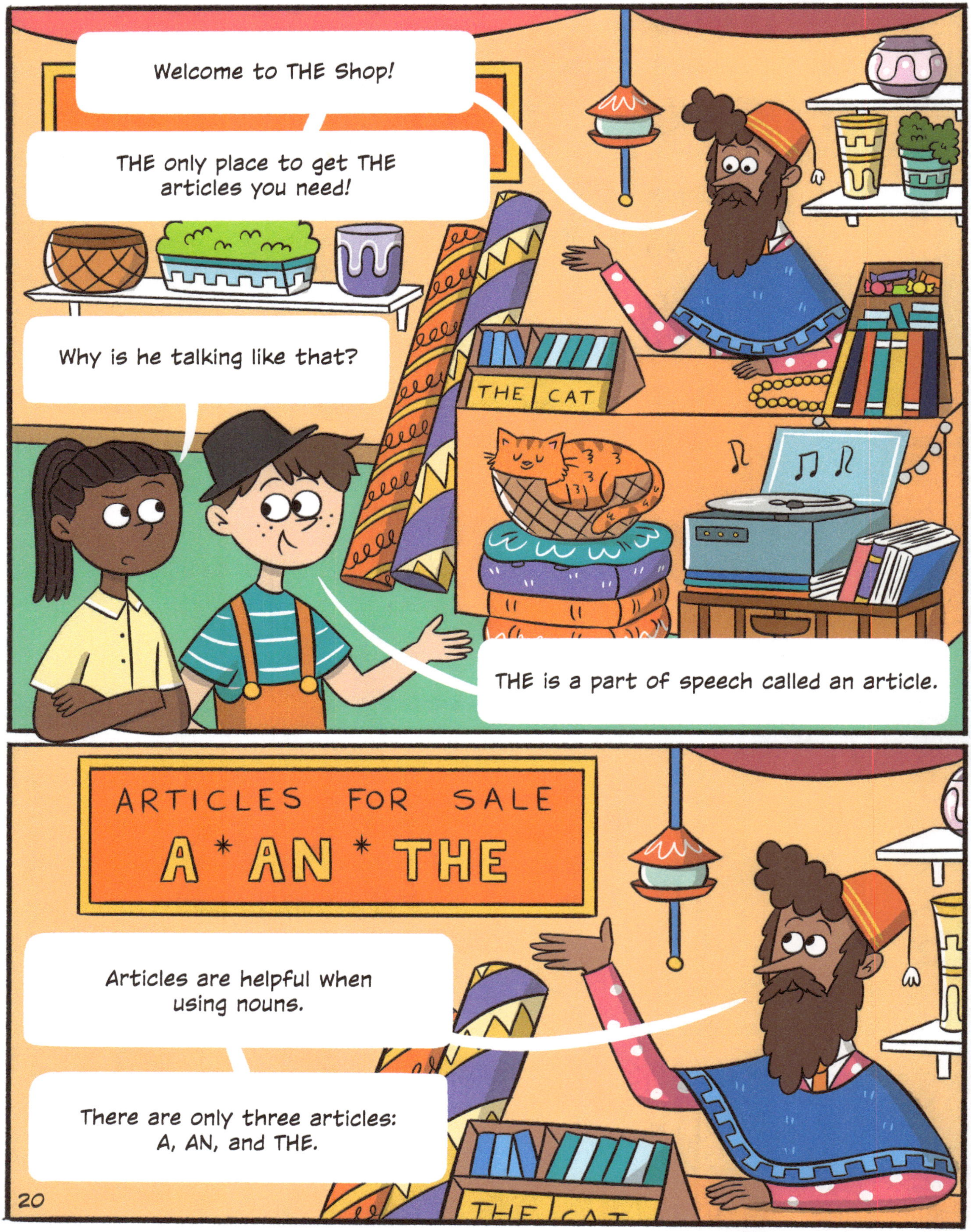
Welcome to THE Shop!
THE only place to get THE articles you need!
Why is he talking like that?
THE is a part of speech called an article.
THE CAT
ARTICLES FOR SALE
A * AN * THE
Articles are helpful when using nouns.
There are only three articles: A, AN, and THE.

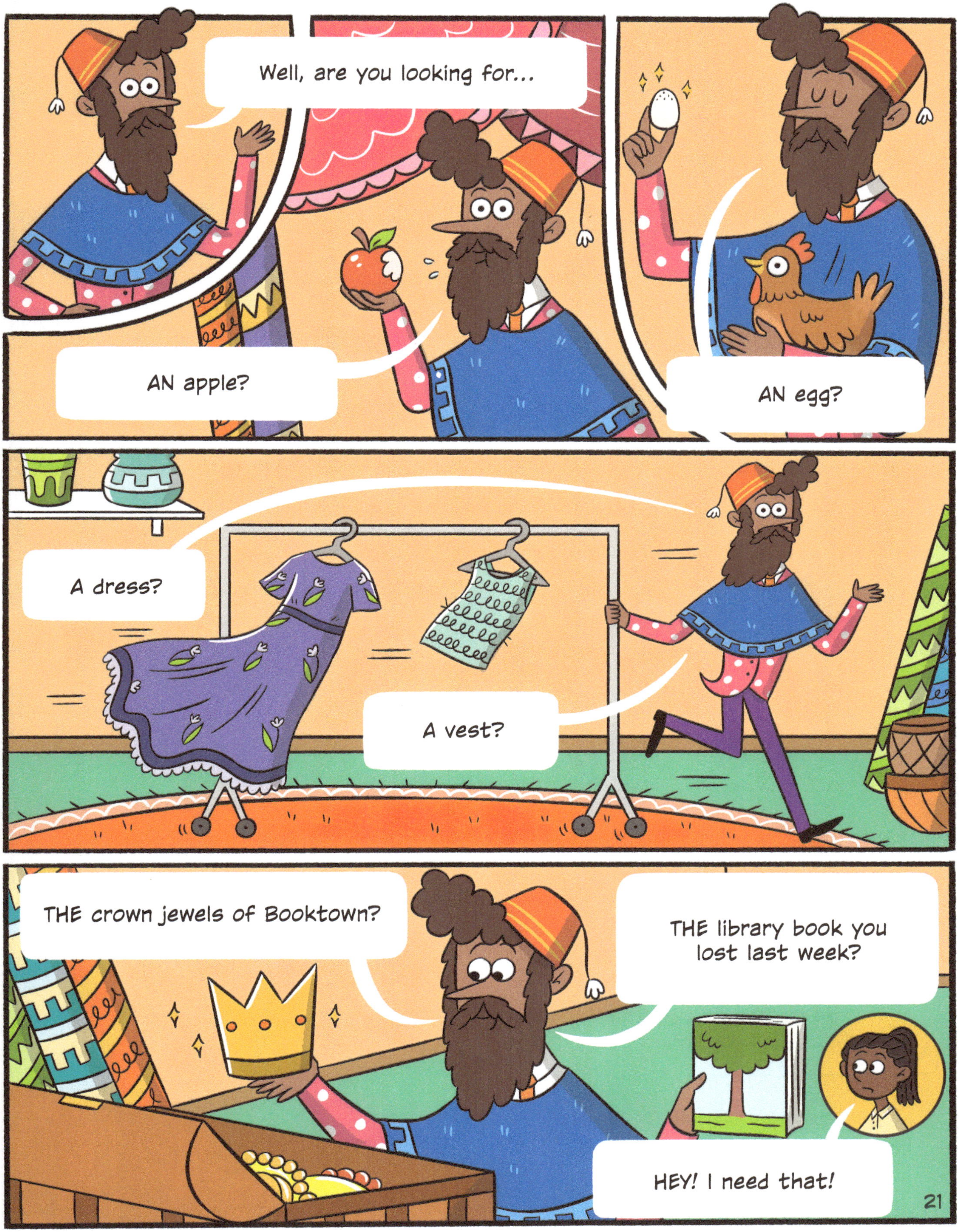
Well, are you looking for...
AN apple?
AN egg?
A dress?
A vest?
THE crown jewels of Booktown?
THE library book you lost last week?
HEY! I need that!

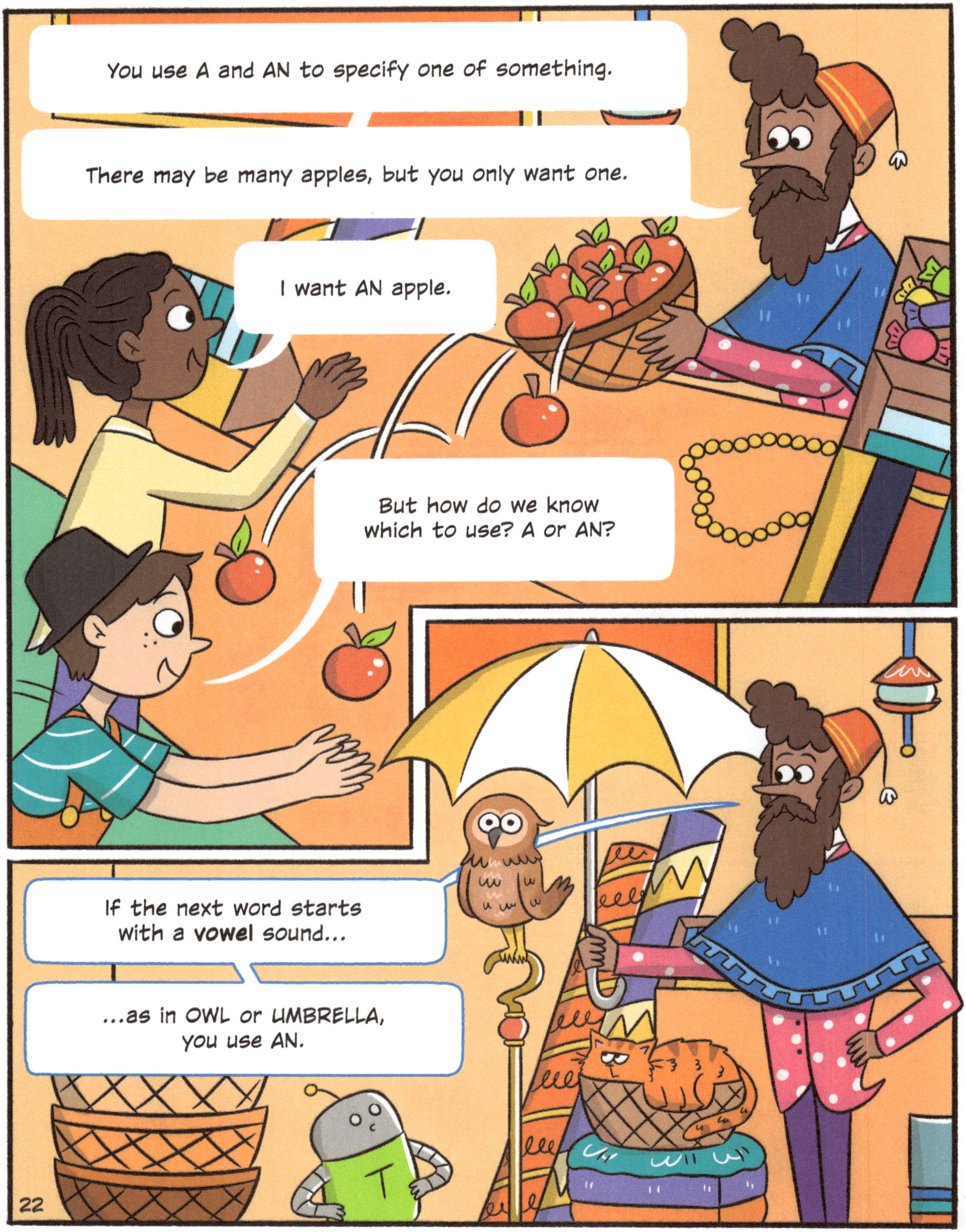
You use A and AN to specify one of something.
There may be many apples, but you only want one.
I want AN apple.
But how do we know which to use? A or AN?
If the next word starts with a **vowel** sound...
...as in OWL or UMBRELLA, you use AN.
T

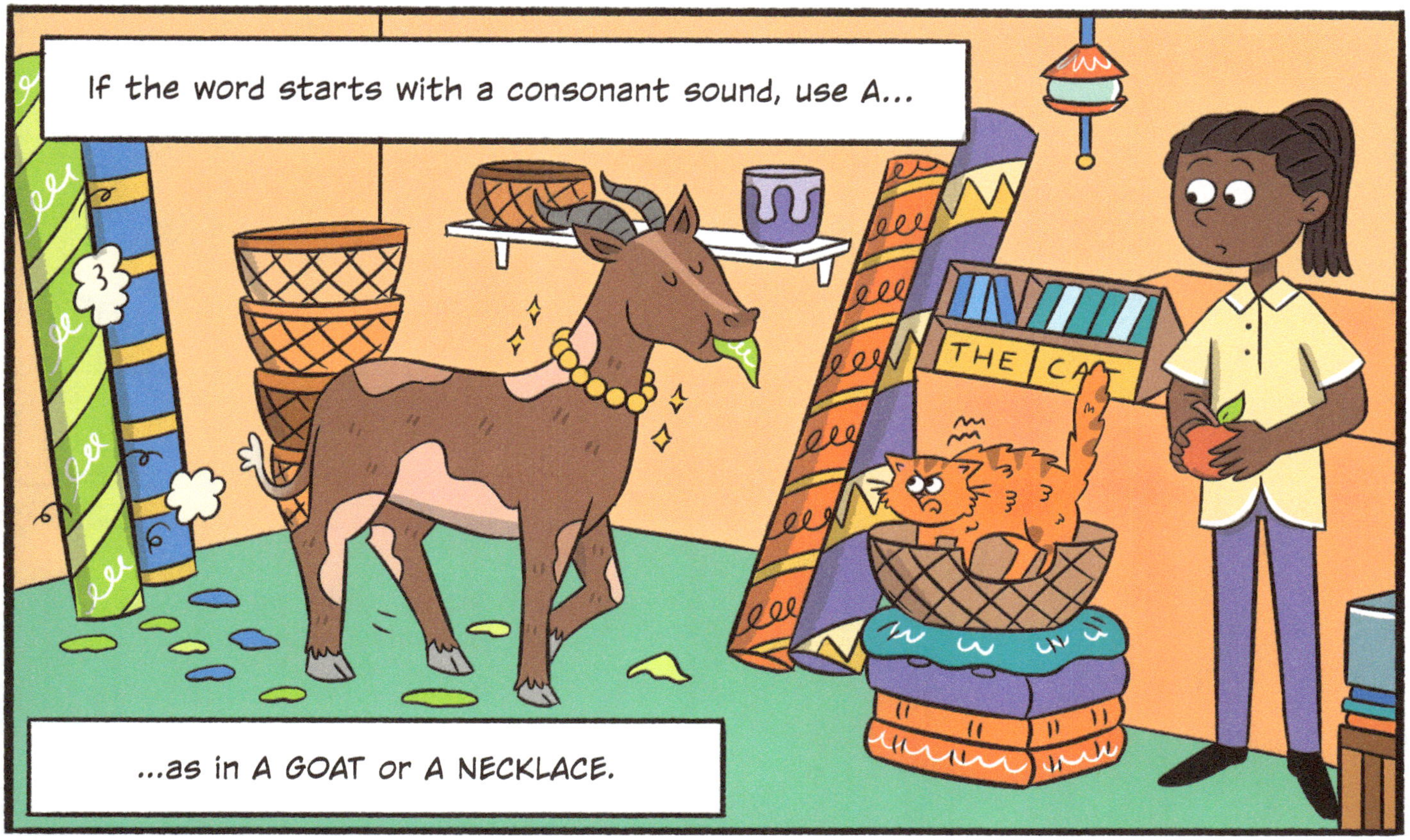
If the word starts with a consonant sound, use A...
THE
...as in A GOAT or A NECKLACE.

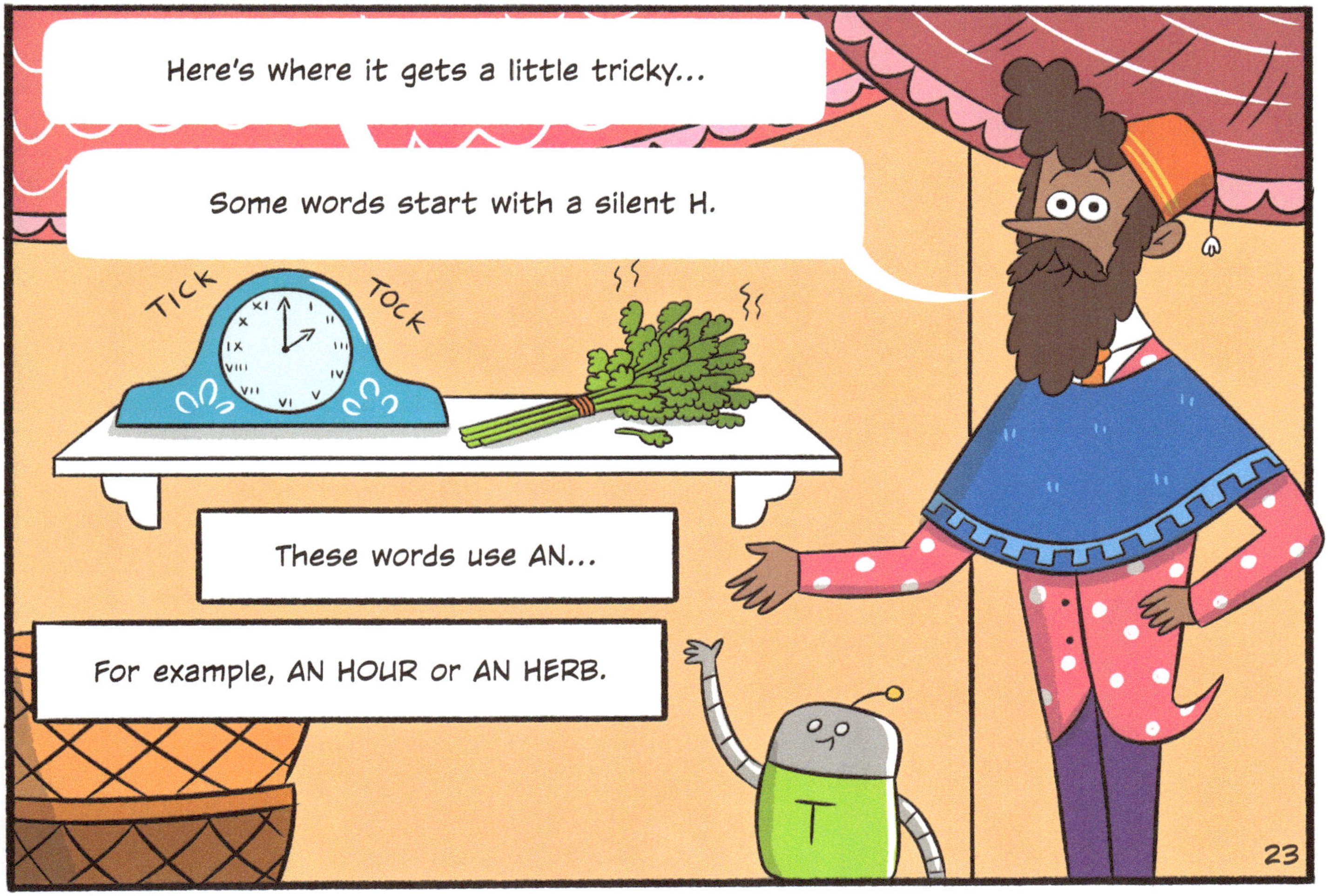
Here's where it gets a little tricky...
Some words start with a silent H.
TICK
TOCK
These words use AN...
For example, AN HOUR or AN HERB.

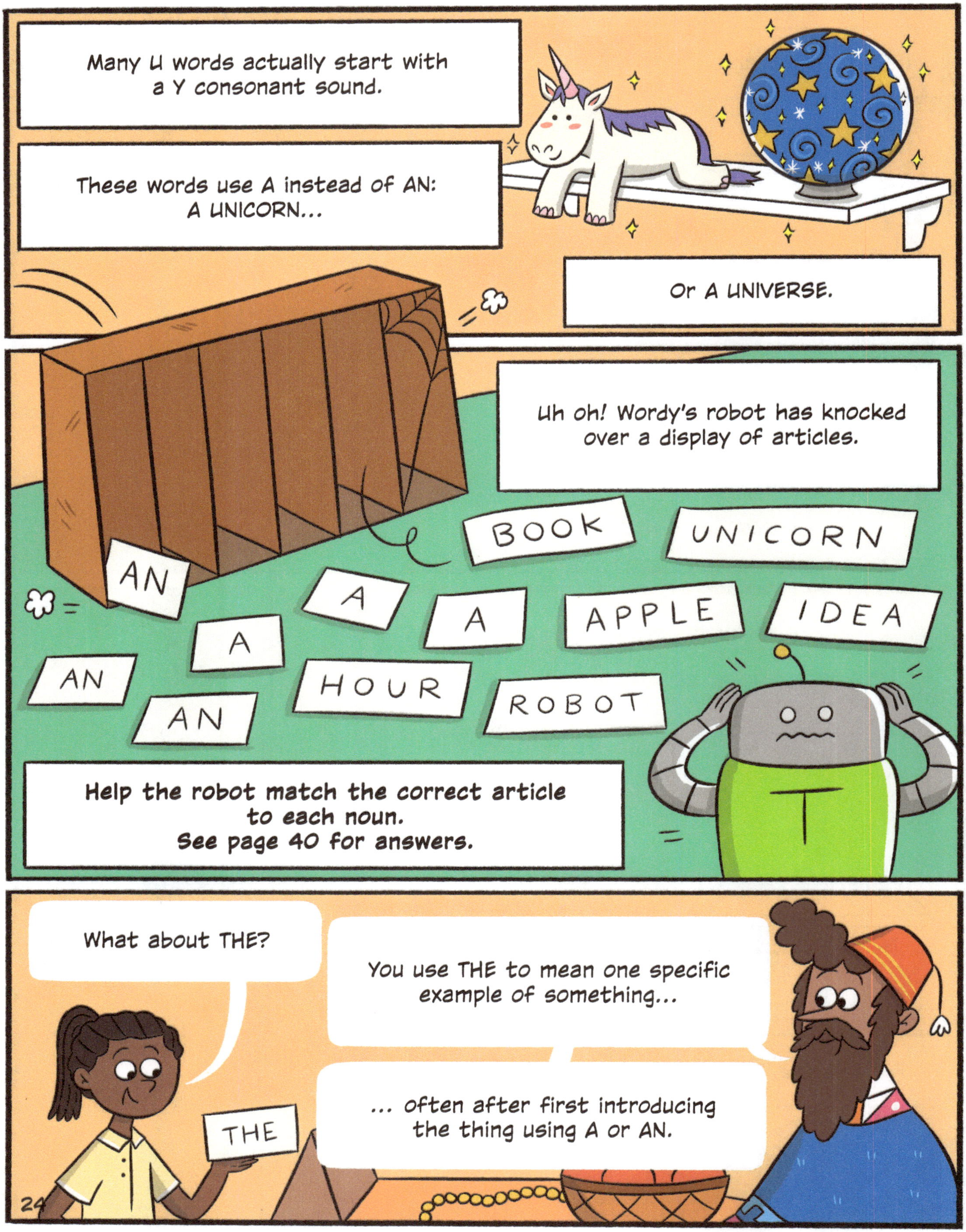
Many U words actually start with a Y consonant sound.
These words use A instead of AN: A UNICORN...
Or A UNIVERSE.
Uh oh! Wordy's robot has knocked over a display of articles.
BOOK
UNICORN
AN
A
A
APPLE
IDEA
A
AN
HOUR
ROBOT
AN
Help the robot match the correct article to each noun. See page 40 for answers.
What about THE?
You use THE to mean one specific example of something...
... often after first introducing the thing using A or AN.
THE

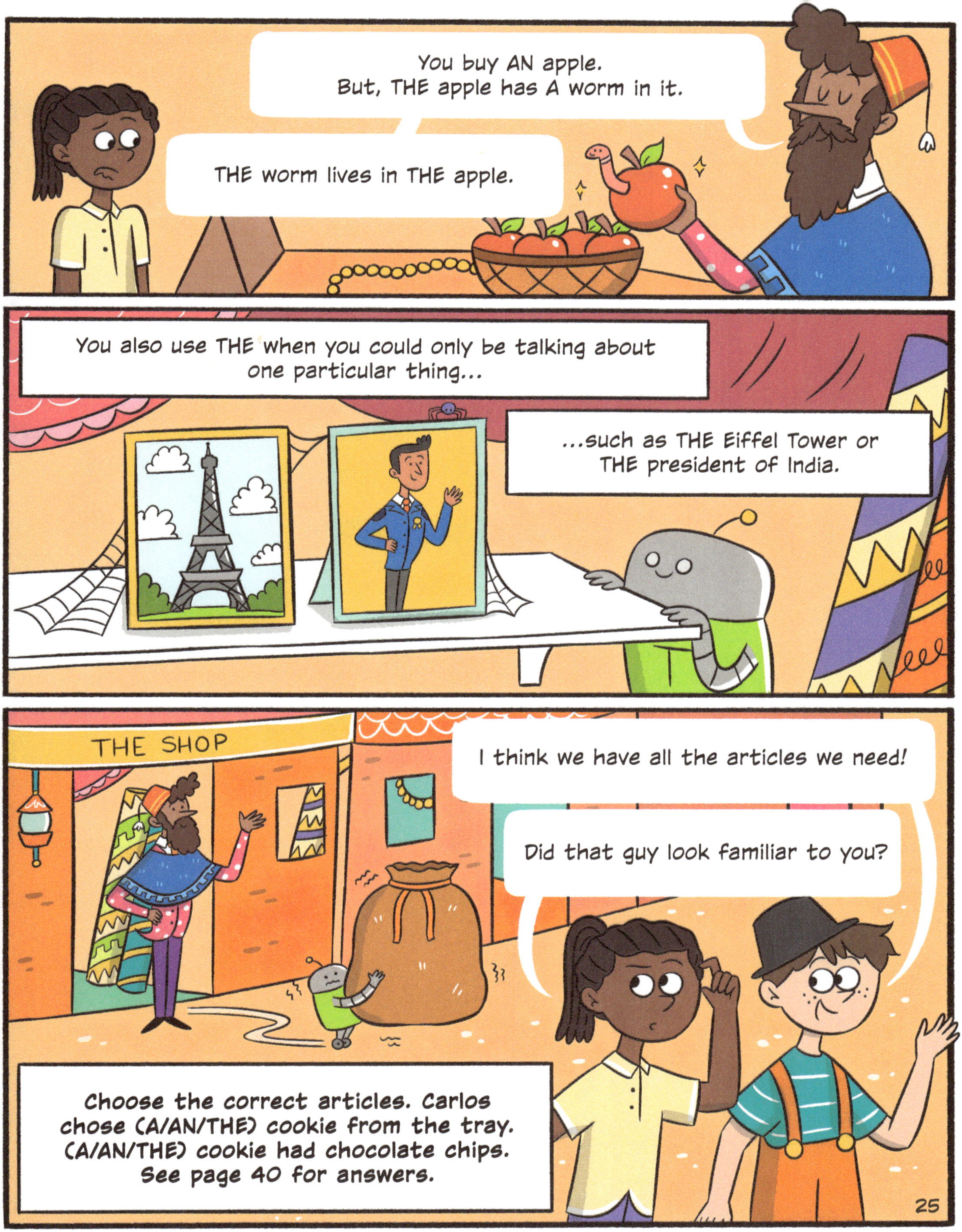
You buy AN apple.
But, THE apple has A worm in it.
THE worm lives in THE apple.
You also use THE when you could only be talking about one particular thing...
...such as THE Eiffel Tower or THE president of India.
THE SHOP
I think we have all the articles we need!
Did that guy look familiar to you?
Choose the correct articles. Carlos chose (A/AN/THE) cookie from the tray. (A/AN/THE) cookie had chocolate chips. See page 40 for answers.

ADVERBS

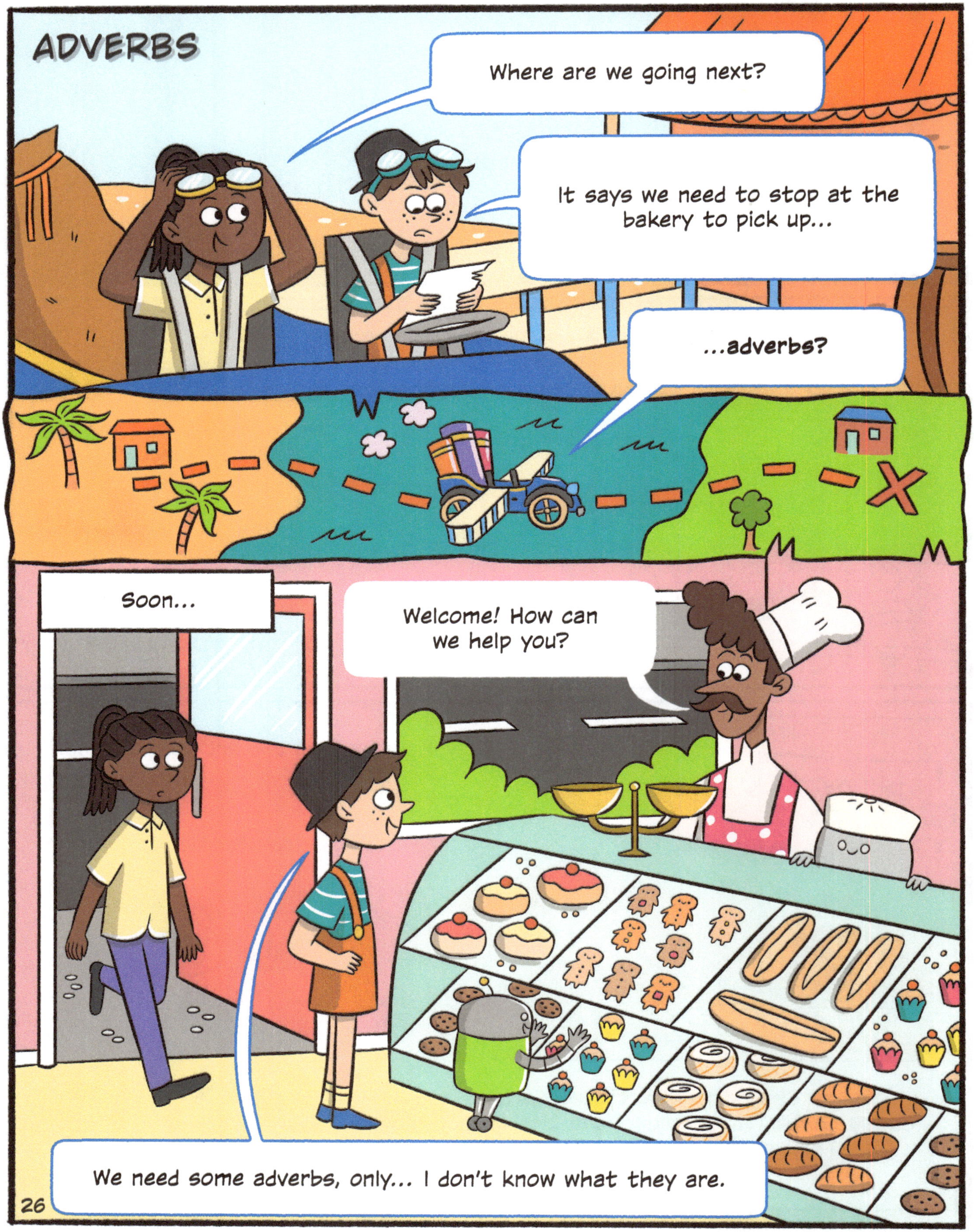

Where are we going next?
It says we need to stop at the bakery to pick up...
...adverbs?
Soon...
Welcome! How can we help you?
We need some adverbs, only... I don't know what they are.

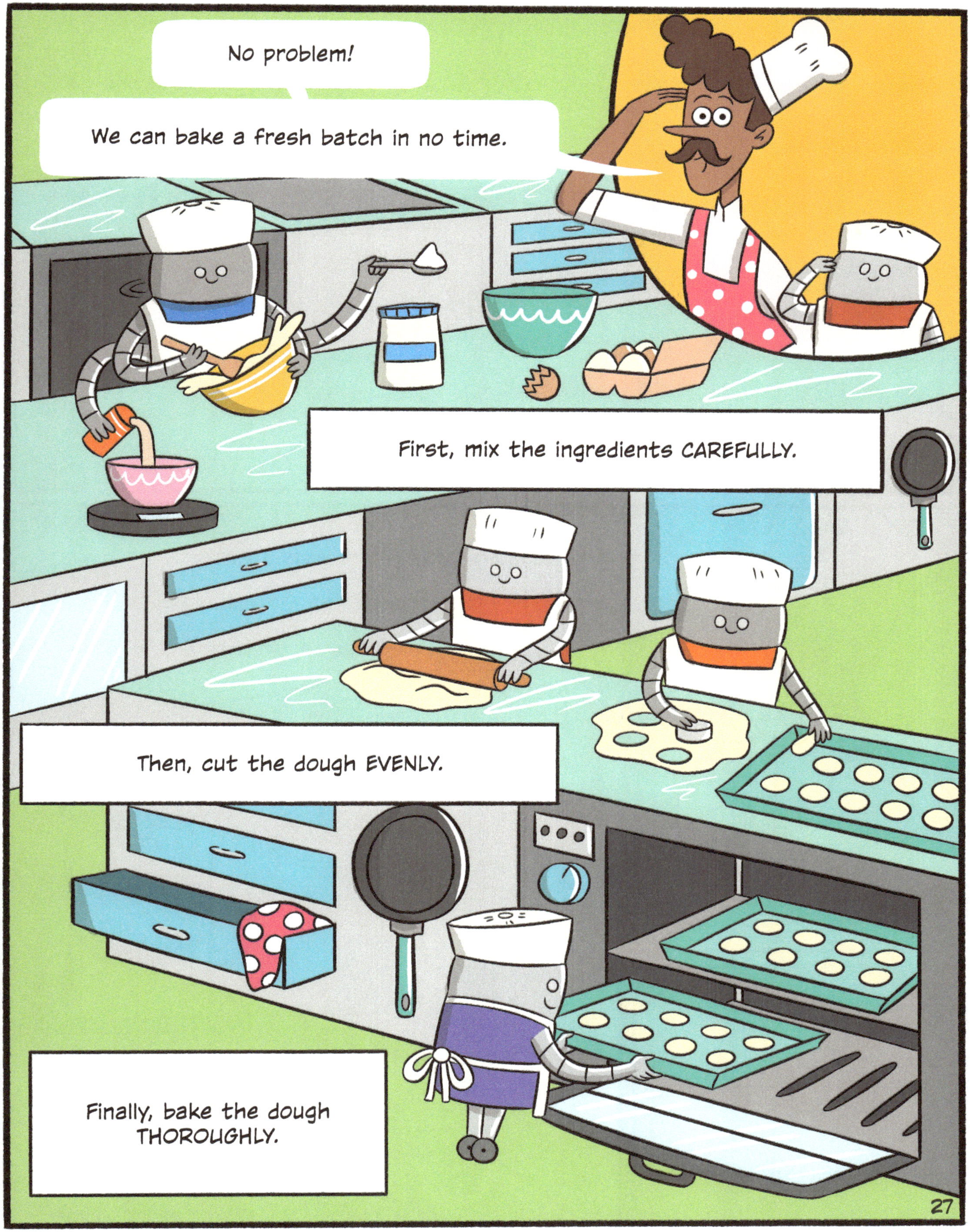
No problem!
We can bake a fresh batch in no time.
First, mix the ingredients CAREFULLY.
Then, cut the dough EVENLY.
Finally, bake the dough THOROUGHLY.

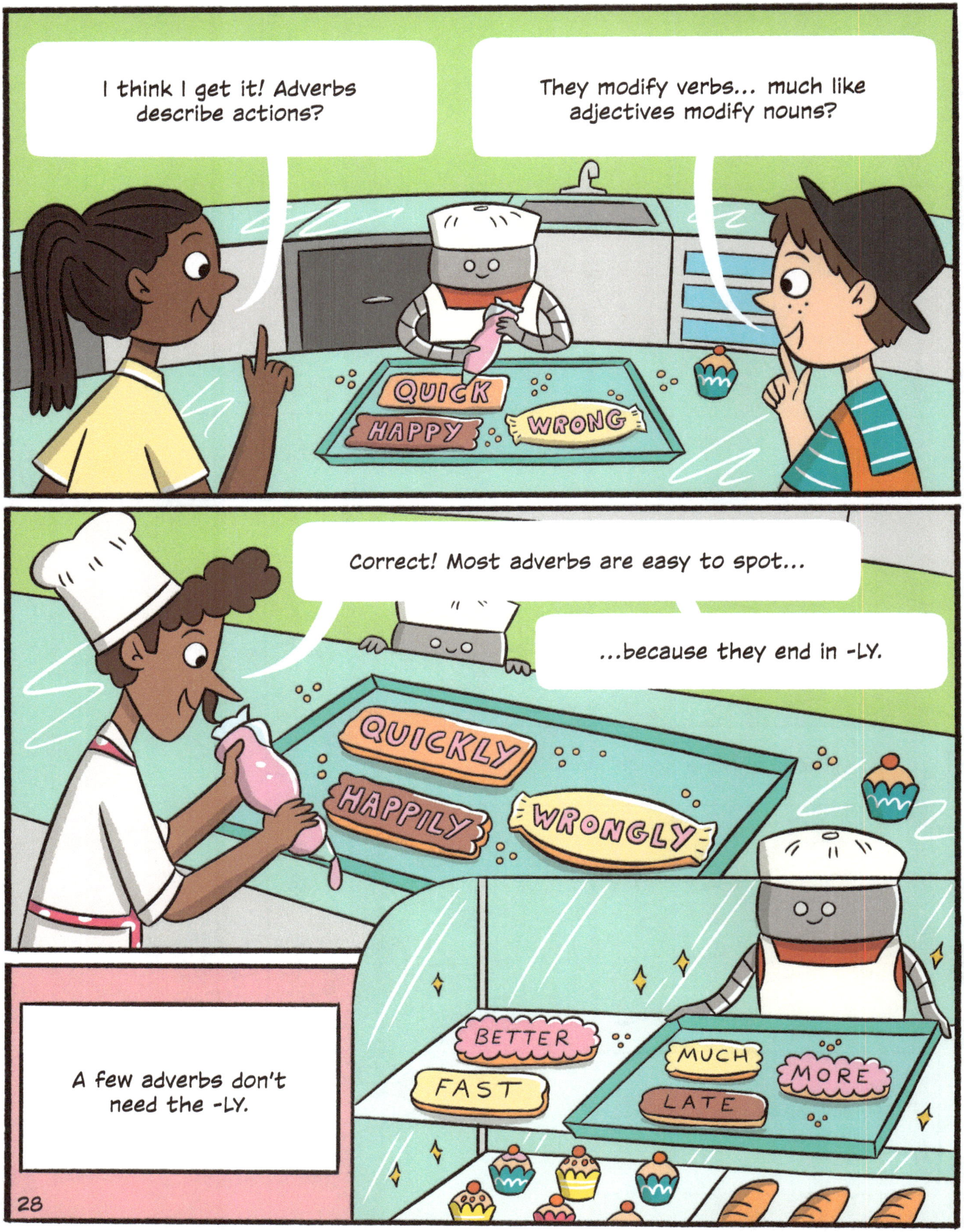
I think I get it! Adverbs describe actions?
They modify verbs... much like adjectives modify nouns?
QUICK
HAPPY
WRONG
Correct! Most adverbs are easy to spot...
...because they end in -LY.
QUICKLY
HAPPILY
WRONGLY
A few adverbs don't need the -LY.
BETTER
FAST
MUCH
MORE
LATE

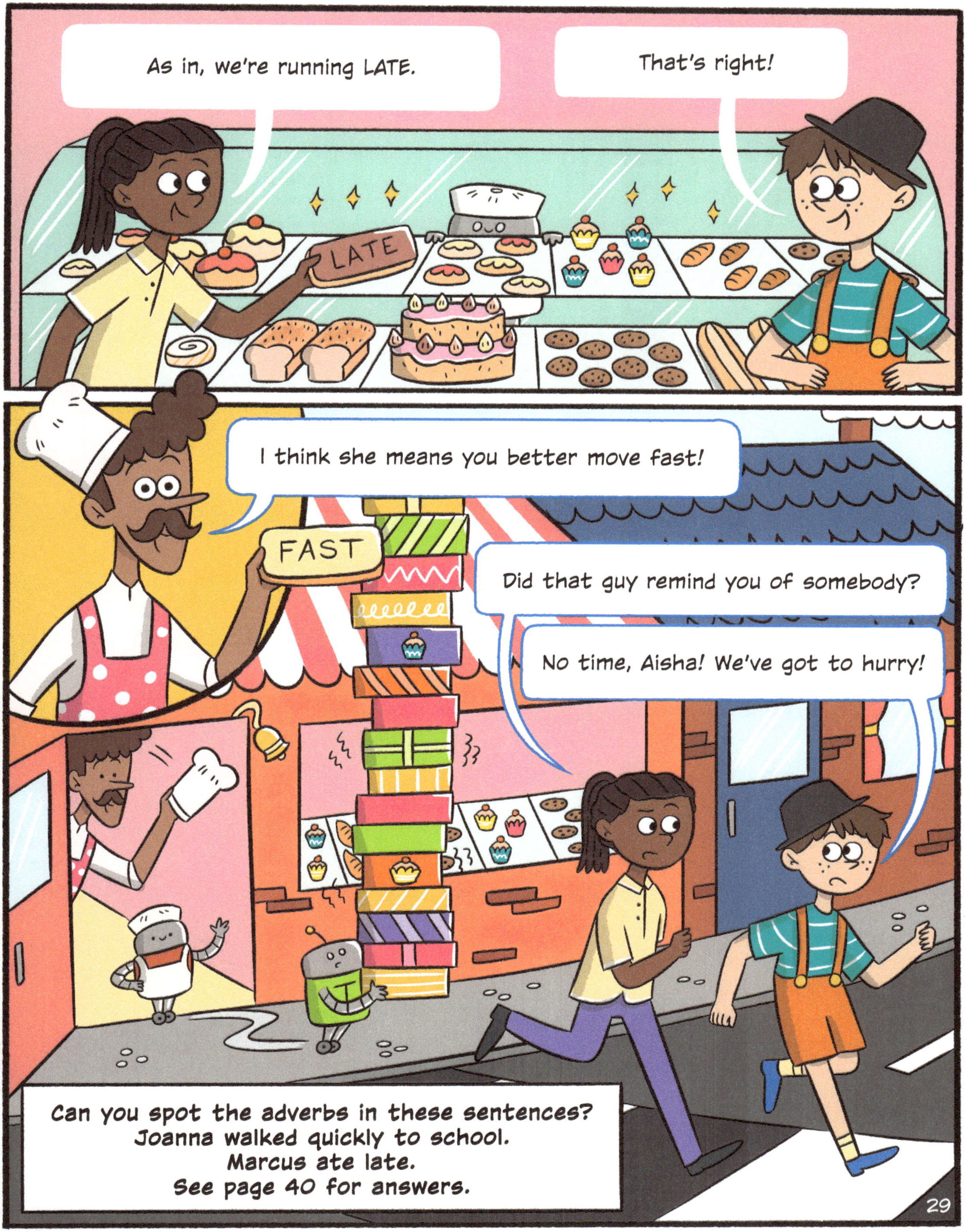
As in, we're running LATE.
That's right!
LATE
I think she means you better move fast!
FAST
Did that guy remind you of somebody?
No time, Aisha! We've got to hurry!
Can you spot the adverbs in these sentences?
Joanna walked quickly to school.
Marcus ate late.
See page 40 for answers.

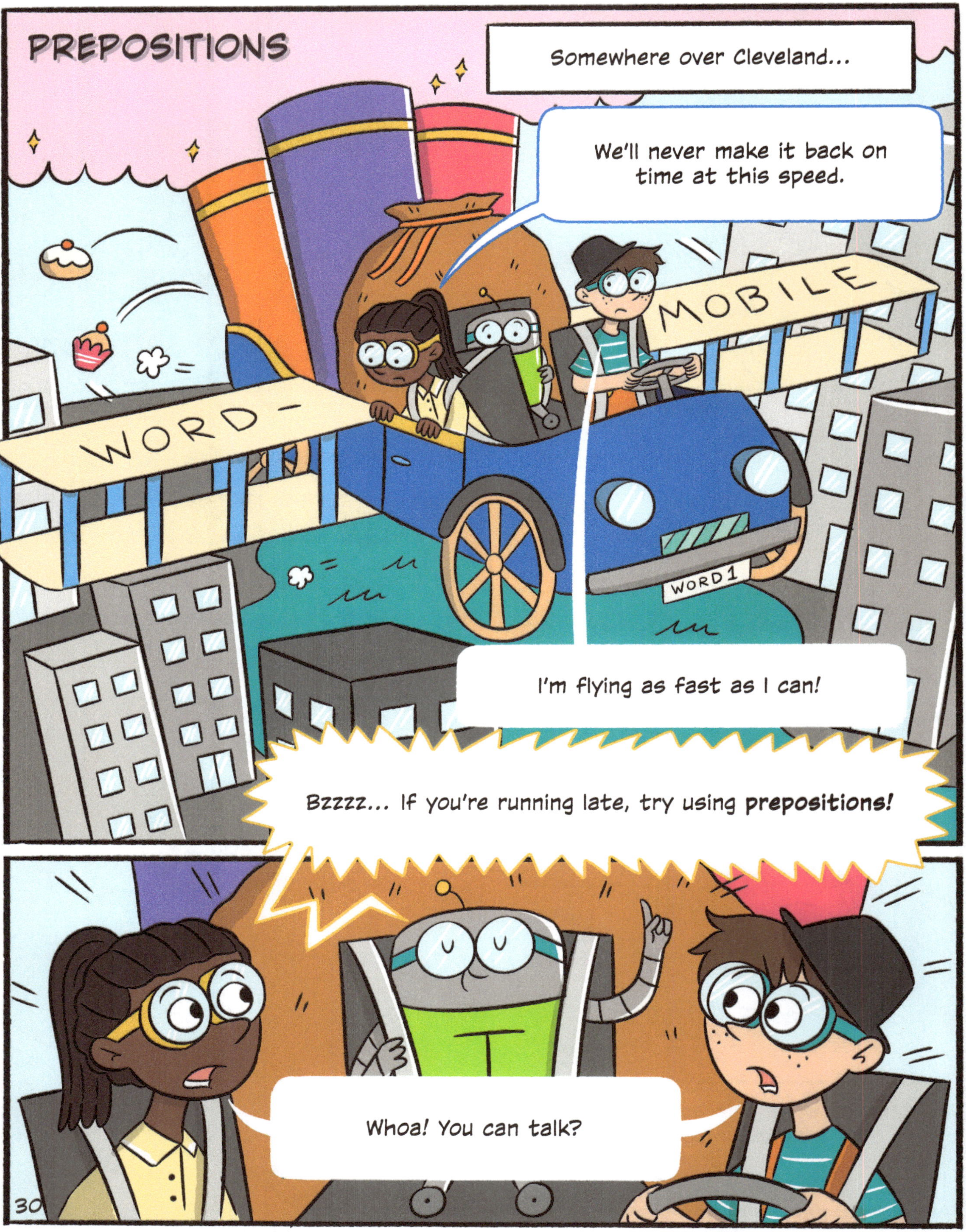
PREPOSITIONS
Somewhere over Cleveland...
We'll never make it back on time at this speed.
WORD-
MOBILE
WORD1
I'm flying as fast as I can!
Bzzzz... If you're running late, try using **prepositions!**
Whoa! You can talk?

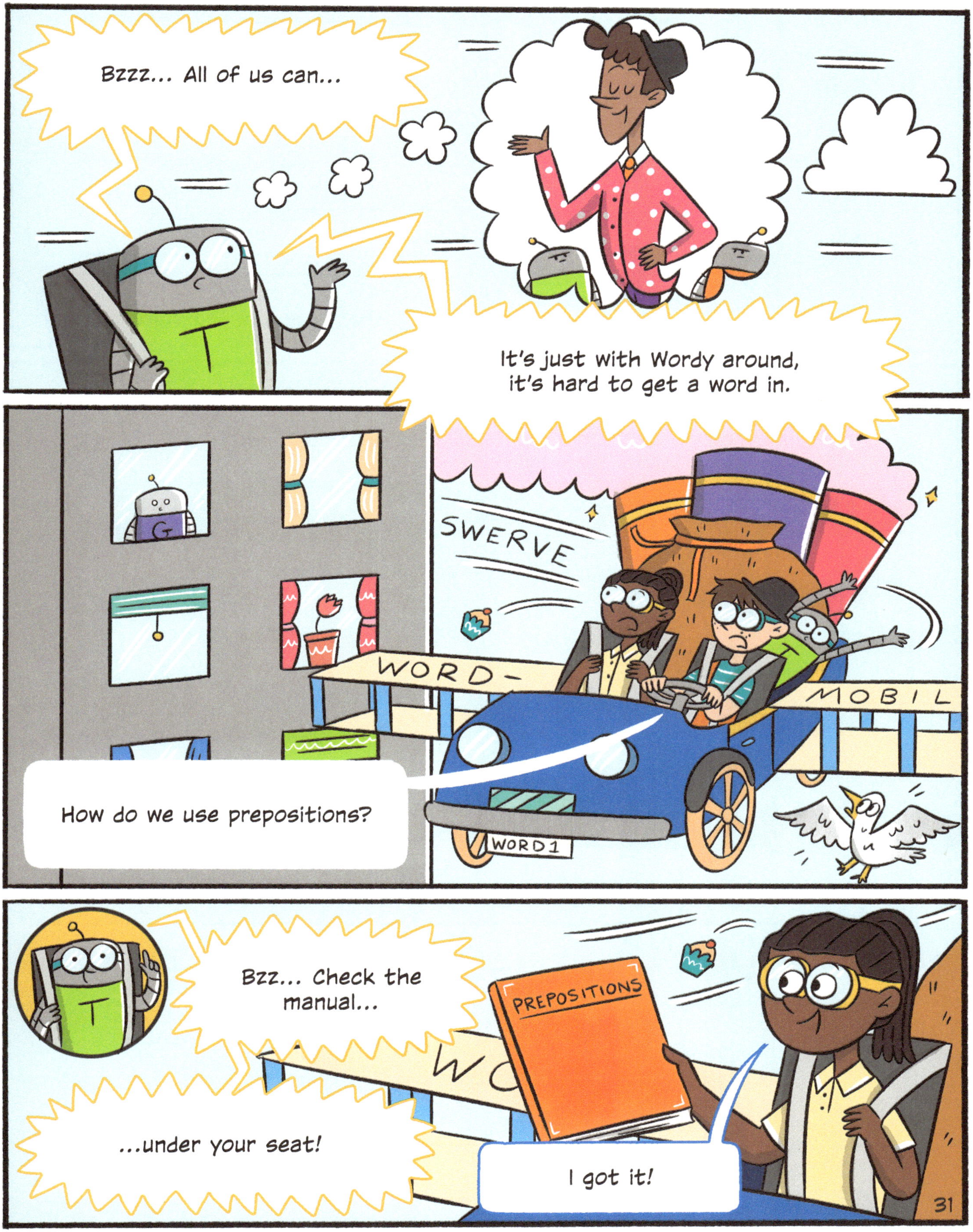
Bzzz... All of us can...
It's just with Wordy around, it's hard to get a word in.
SWERVE
WORD-
MOBIL
WORD1
How do we use prepositions?
Bzz... Check the manual...
...under your seat!
PREPOSITIONS
I got it!

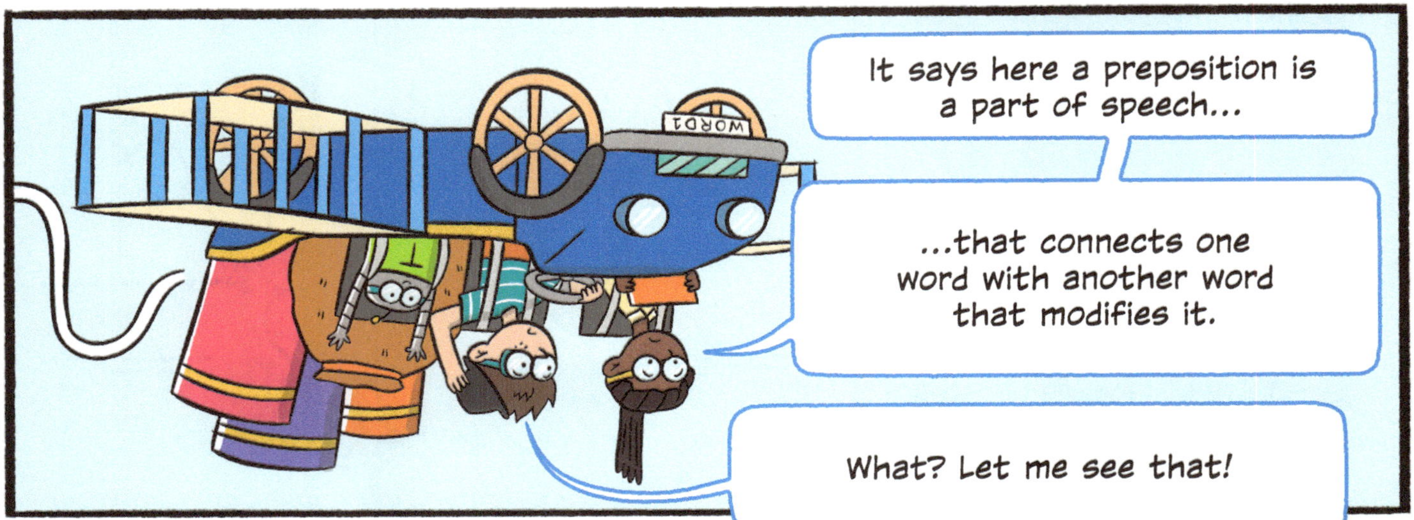
It says here a preposition is a part of speech...
...that connects one word with another word that modifies it.
What? Let me see that!

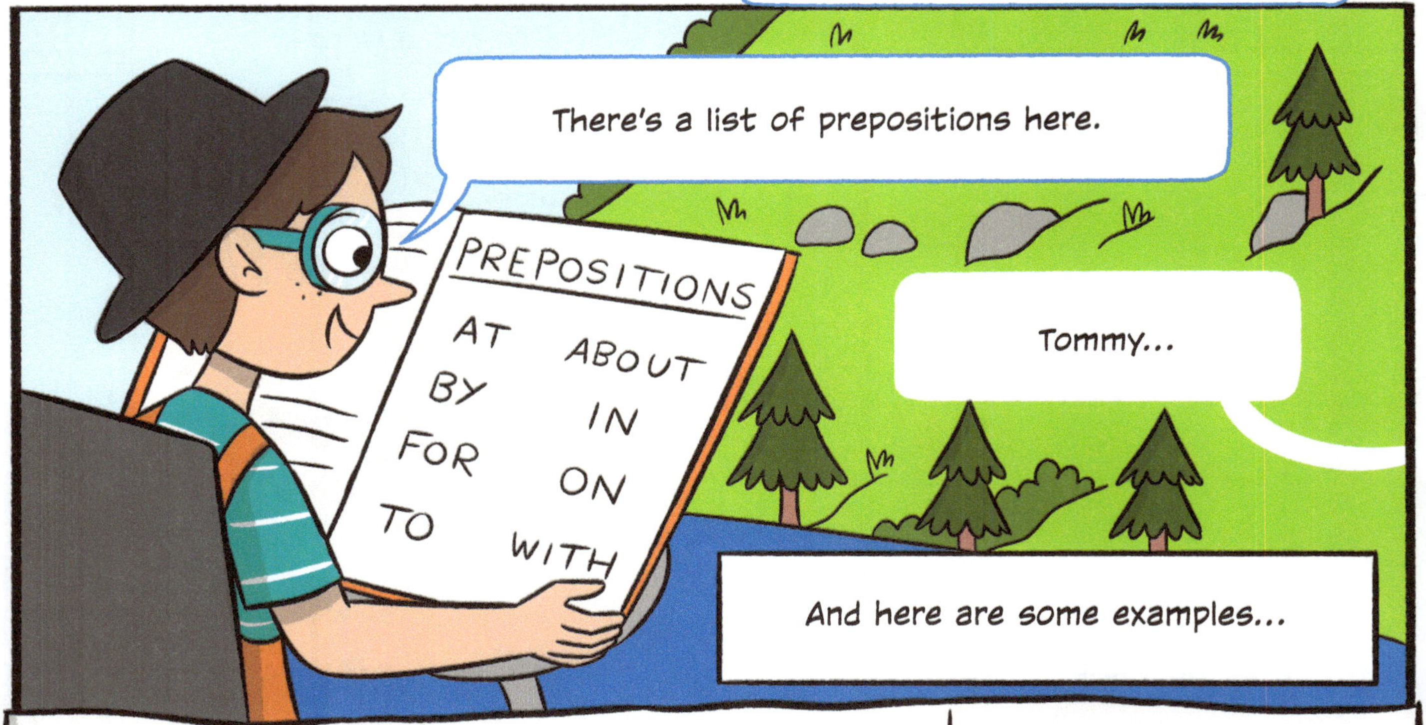
There's a list of prepositions here.
PREPOSITIONS
AT
BY
FOR
TO
ABOUT
IN
ON
WITH
Tommy...
And here are some examples...

WORD	PREPOSITION	OBJECT
The girl	in	the dress
A letter	for	Tommy
Run	to	the store

TOMMY!

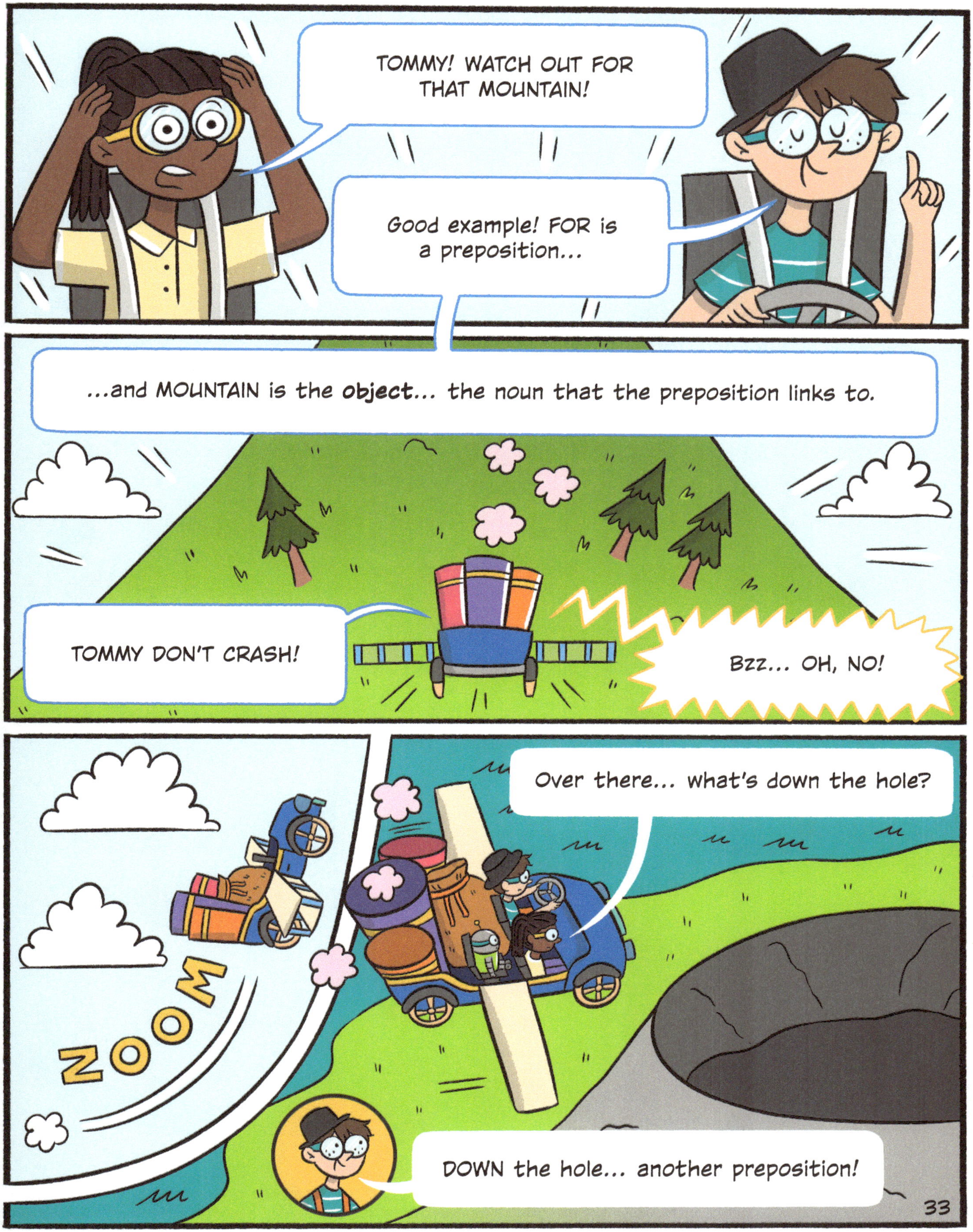

TOMMY! WATCH OUT FOR THAT MOUNTAIN!
Good example! FOR is a preposition...
...and MOUNTAIN is the **object**... the noun that the preposition links to.
TOMMY DON'T CRASH!
Bzz... OH, NO!
ZOOM
Over there... what's down the hole?
DOWN the hole... another preposition!

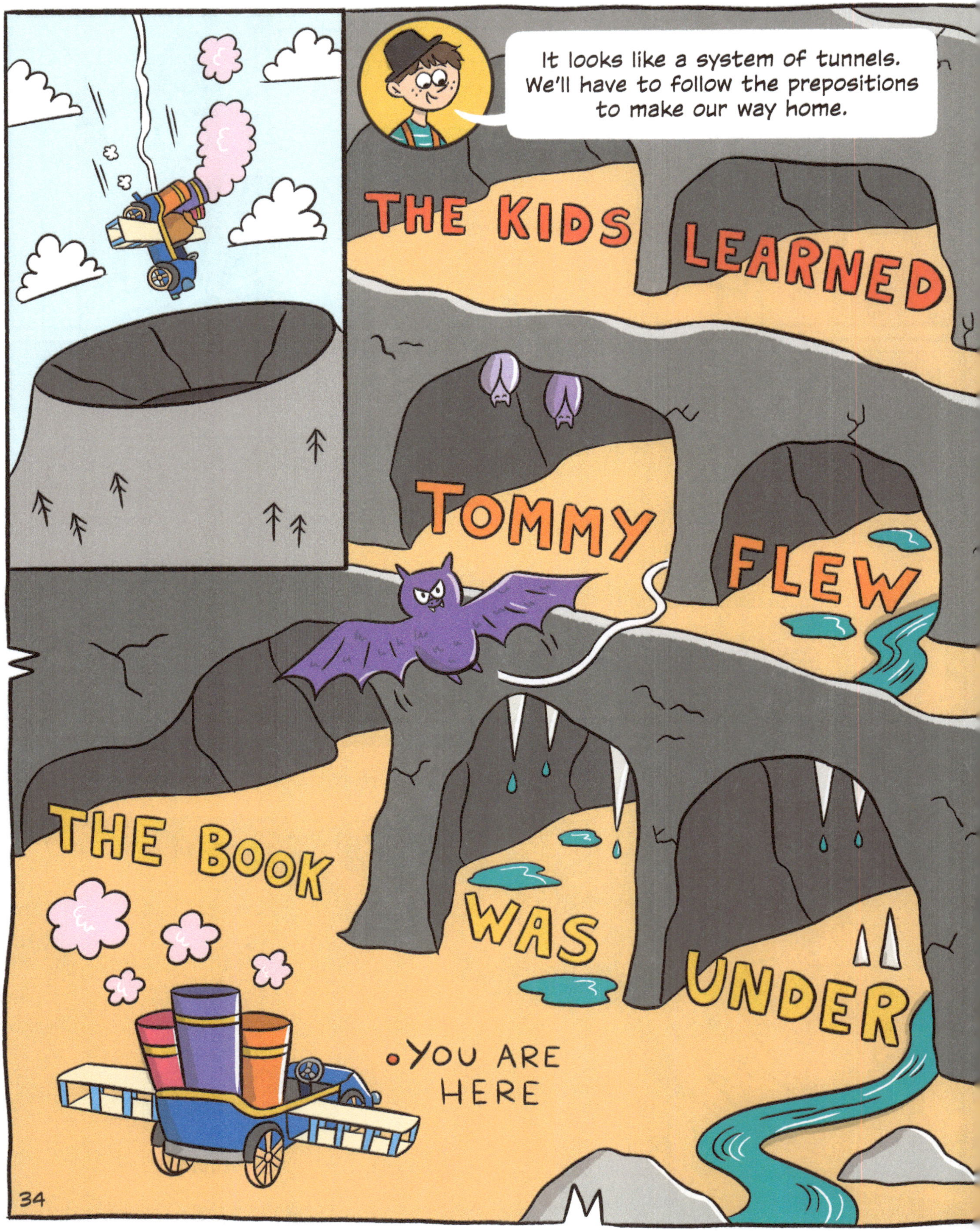

It looks like a system of tunnels. We'll have to follow the prepositions to make our way home.
THE KIDS
LEARNED
TOMMY
FLEW
THE BOOK
WAS
UNDER
YOU ARE HERE

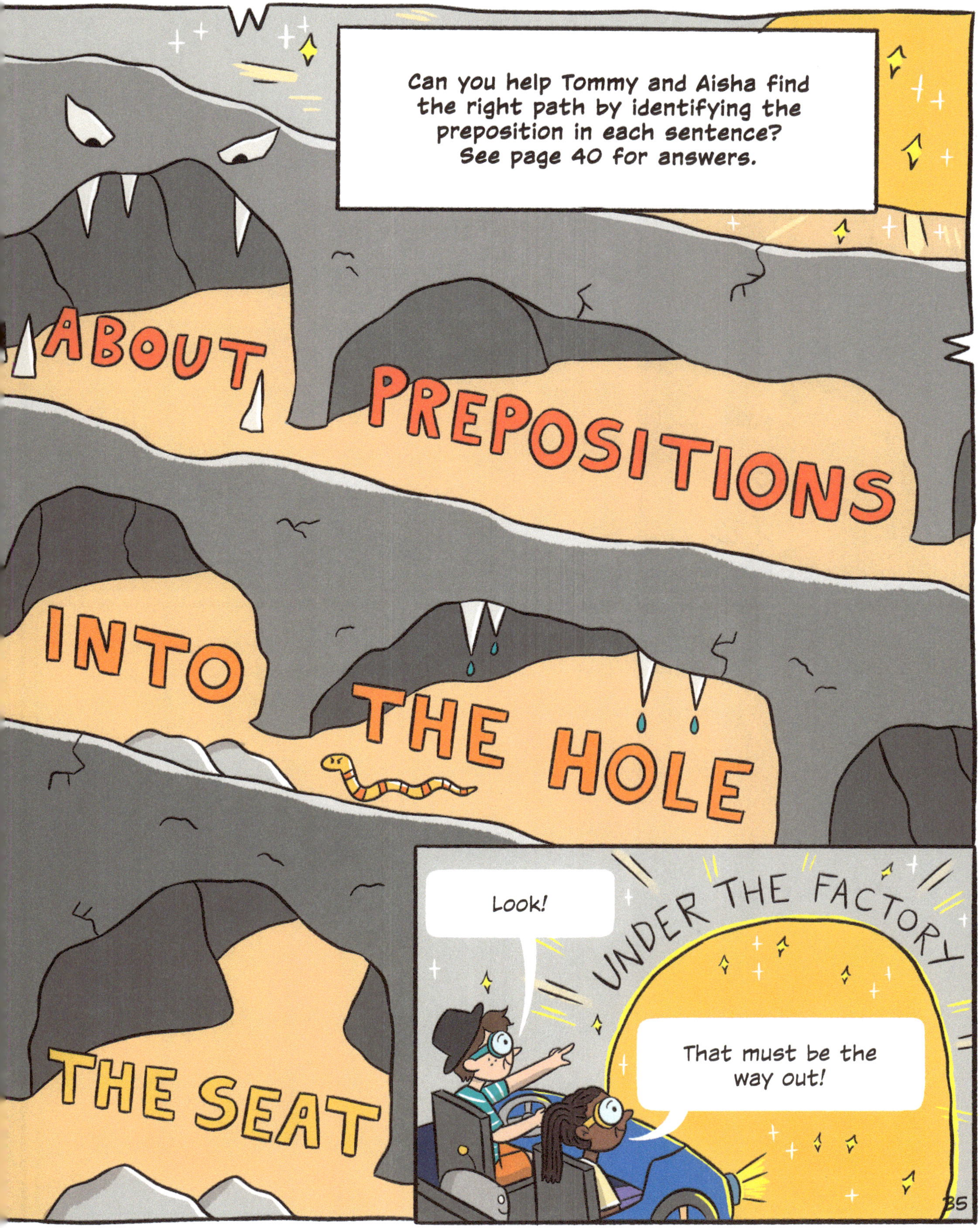
Can you help Tommy and Aisha find the right path by identifying the preposition in each sentence? See page 40 for answers.
ABOUT PREPOSITIONS
INTO THE HOLE
THE SEAT
UNDER THE FACTORY
Look!
That must be the way out!

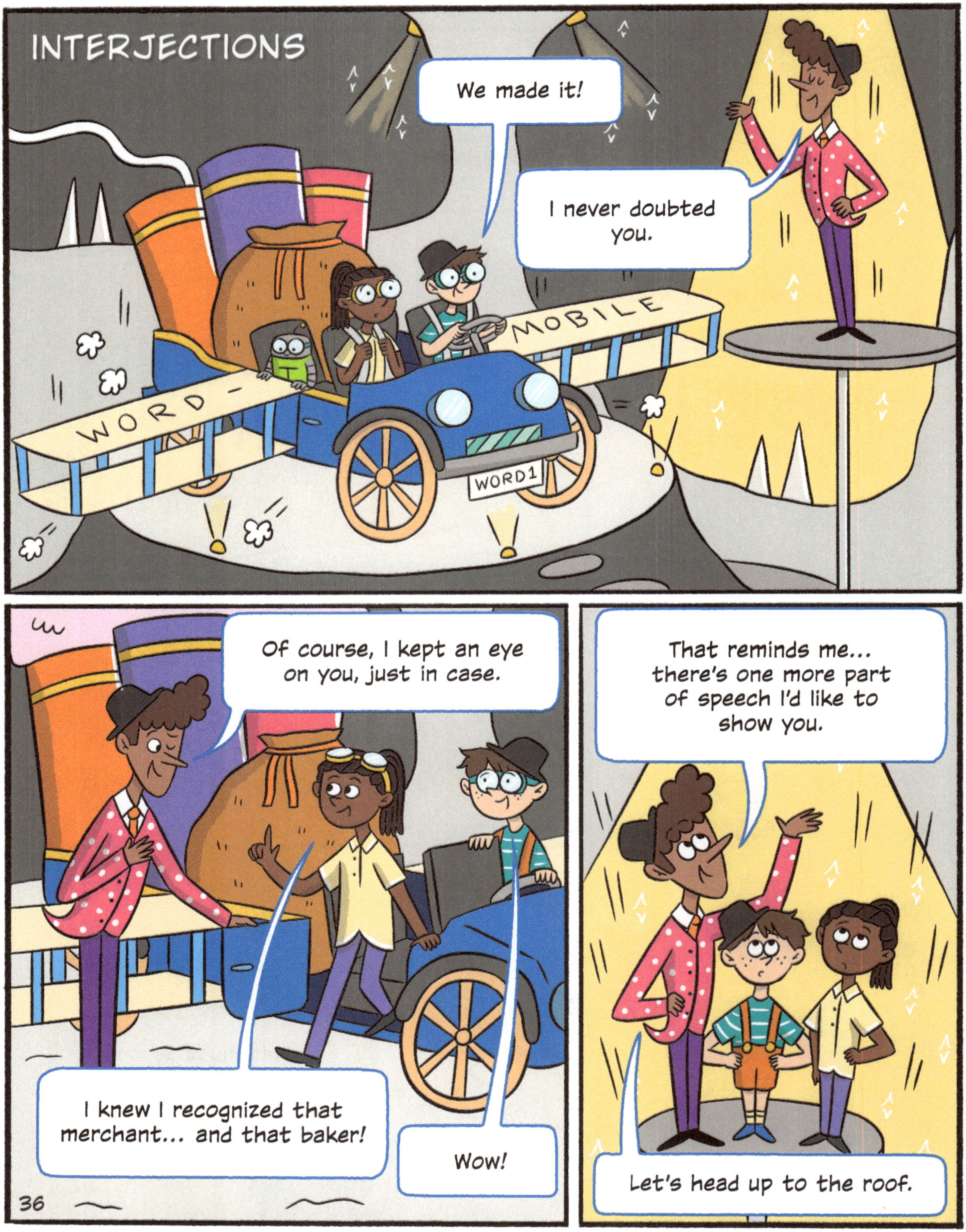
INTERJECTIONS
We made it!
I never doubted you.
WORD-MOBILE
WORD1
Of course, I kept an eye on you, just in case.
I knew I recognized that merchant... and that baker!
Wow!
That reminds me... there's one more part of speech I'd like to show you.
Let's head up to the roof.

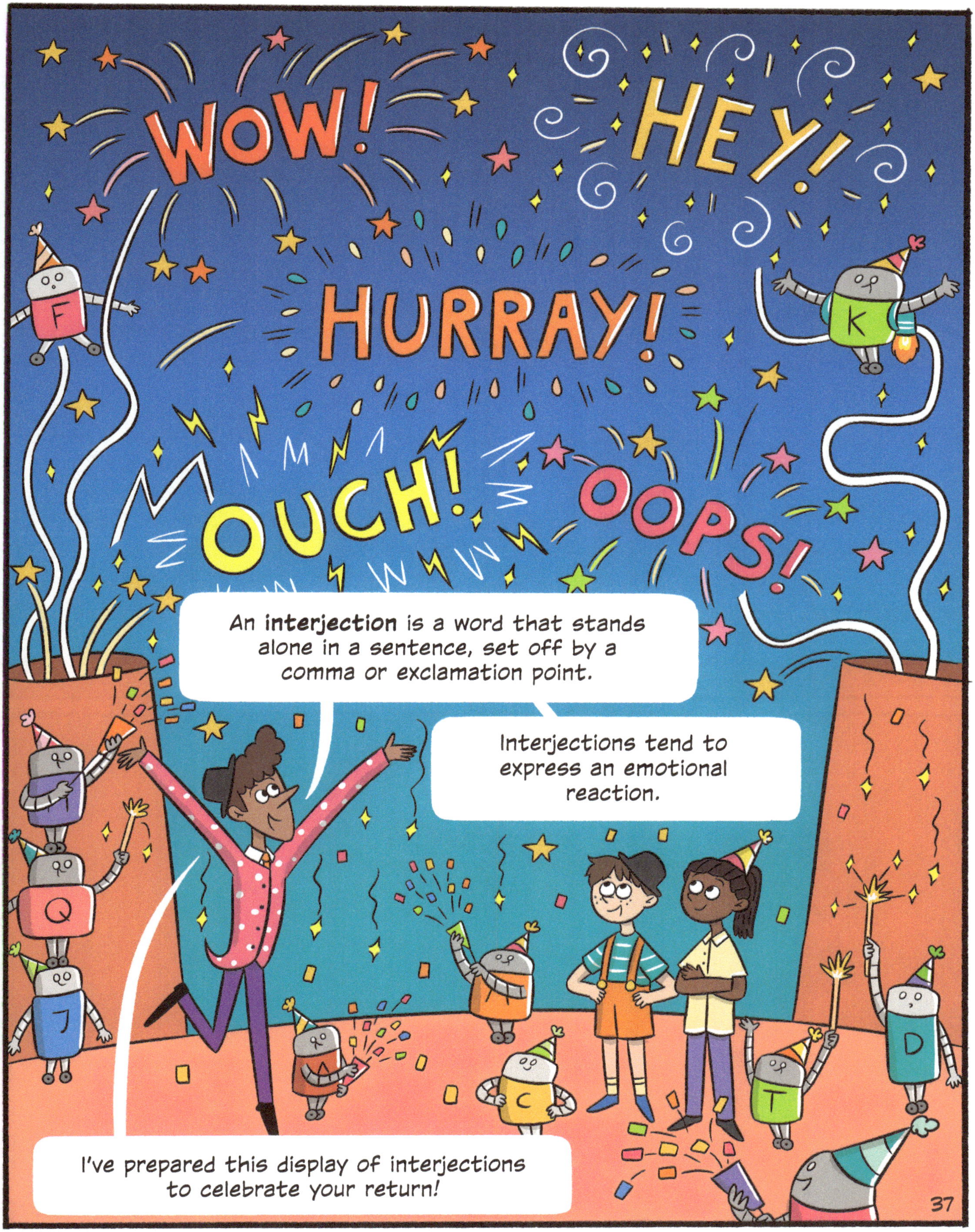
WOW!
HEY!
HURRAY!
OUCH!
OOPS!
An **interjection** is a word that stands alone in a sentence, set off by a comma or exclamation point.
Interjections tend to express an emotional reaction.
I've prepared this display of interjections to celebrate your return!

SHOW WHAT YOU KNOW

1. Can you find the adjectives in the following?

A. The little girl wanted a pink pony.
B. The green snake slithered by.
C. We saw tall trees and shiny rocks.

2. Identify the preposition and object in each sentence.

A. The parade marched down the street.
B. Marco watched a movie about superheroes.
C. Dad put dinner on the table early.

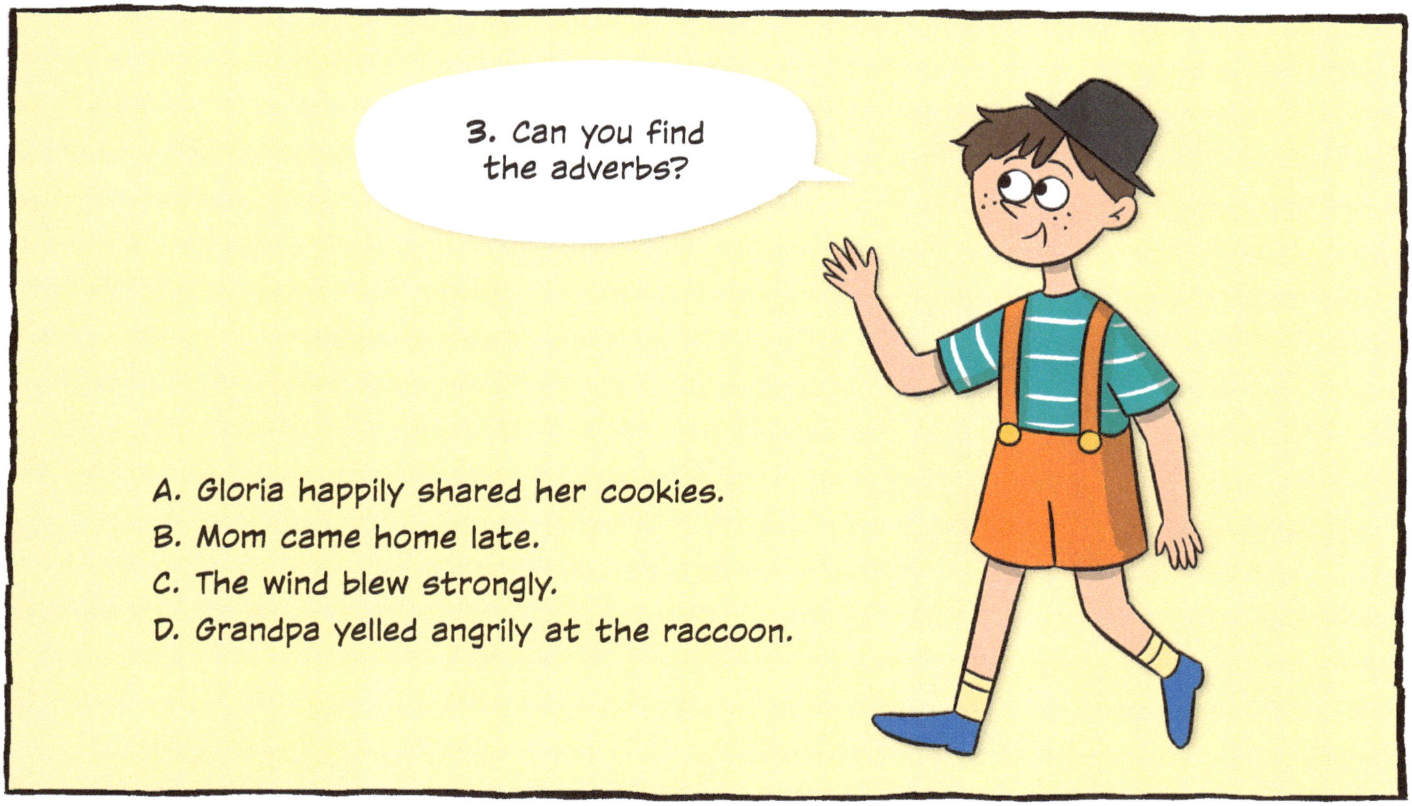
3. Can you find the adverbs?
A. Gloria happily shared her cookies.
B. Mom came home late.
C. The wind blew strongly.
D. Grandpa yelled angrily at the raccoon.

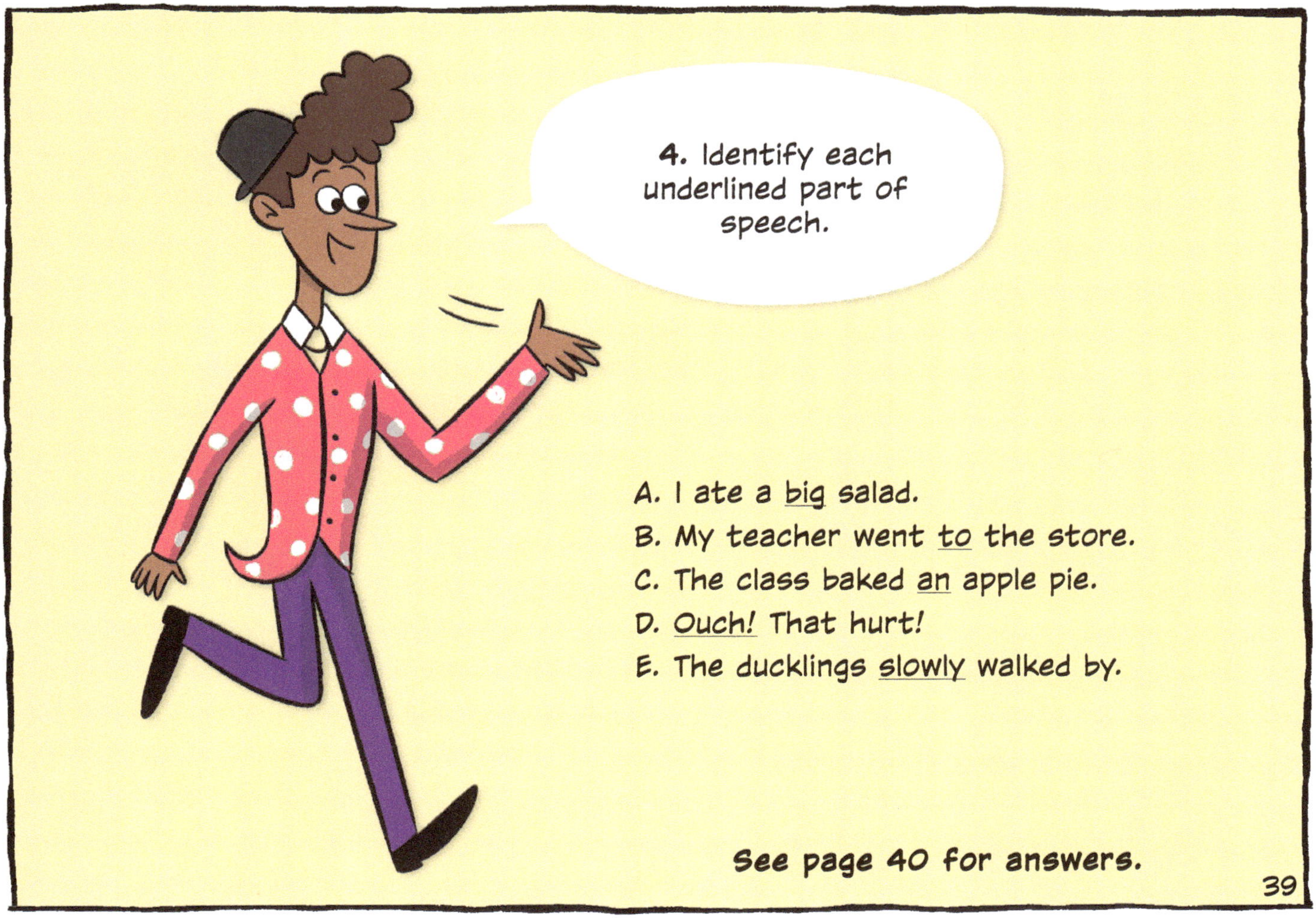
4. Identify each underlined part of speech.
A. I ate a big salad.
B. My teacher went to the store.
C. The class baked an apple pie.
D. Ouch! That hurt!
E. The ducklings slowly walked by.

See page 40 for answers.

ANSWERS

page 11: BROWN, LONG
HUNGRY, GOOD
OTHER

page 15:
RED, REDDER, REDDEST
ICY, ICIER, ICIEST
DIFFICULT, MORE DIFFICULT, MOST DIFFICULT

page 24: That child clinging to O looked a lot like Y. I wonder what he was doing there?

page 21: A BOOK
A UNICORN
AN APPLE
AN IDEA
AN HOUR
A ROBOT

page 25: Carlos chose A cookie from the tray. THE cookie had chocolate chips.

page 29: QUICKLY, LATE

page 34 and 35:
The book was <u>under</u> the seat.
Tommy flew <u>into</u> the hole.
The kids learned <u>about</u> prepositions.

SHOW WHAT YOU KNOW ANSWERS
pages 38-39:

1. A. LITTLE, PINK
   B. GREEN
   C. TALL, SHINY

2. Preposition   Object
   A. DOWN   STREET
   B. ABOUT   SUPERHEROES
   C. ON   TABLE

3. A. HAPPILY
   B. LATE
   C. STRONGLY
   D. ANGRILY

4. A. adjective
   B. preposition
   C. article
   D. interjection
   E. adverb

WORDS TO KNOW

adjective a word that *modifies* (changes) the meaning of a noun

adverb a word that *modifies* (changes) the meaning of a verb

article a word used to introduce a noun. The articles are A, AN, and THE.

consonant a sound made by stopping or slowing the breath with tongue, teeth, or lips

interjection a word that stands alone in a sentence, often expressing surprise or emotion

noun a word that refers to a person, place, or thing

object (of a preposition) a word that the preposition connects to the word the preposition *modifies* (changes)

preposition a part of speech that connects a word to another word that *modifies* (changes) it

syllable a word or part of a word pronounced as a single unit